From Hope to Wholeness:

A Presbyterian Response to the Unrest in Baltimore

in April 2015

Baltimore Presbytery
of
The Presbyterian Church
(USA)

Parson's Porch Books

From Hope to Wholeness: A Presbyterian Response to the Unrest in Baltimore in April 2015

ISBN: Softcover 978-0692723272

Copyright © 2016 by John V. Carlson

All rights reserved. No part of this book may be reproduced or transmitted in any form or by any means, electronic or mechanical, including photocopying, recording, or by any information storage and retrieval system, without permission in writing from the publisher.

Cover Photo Credit: Photo of Prayer March taken by Deborah I. Greene.

To order additional copies of this book, contact:

Parson's Porch Books
1-423-475-7308
www.parsonsporch.com

Parson's Porch Books is an imprint of Parson's Porch & Company (PP&C) in Cleveland, Tennessee. PP&C is an innovative company which raises money by publishing books of noted authors, representing all genres. All donations from contributors and profits from publishing are shared with the poor.

From Hope to Wholeness

Table of Contents

Foreword   9

Section I: A Response of Prayer

Loving My Neighbor for Christ: A Call to Prayer   15
(Tanya S. Wade)

A Litany for the City   18
(Carrie Finch-Burriss)

Prayer for Justice   20
(James B. Parks)

A Prayer of Confession for the City of Baltimore   20
(Ronnie A. Hankins)

Two Facets of Justice   28
(Renee Mackey)

Personal Note: Baltimore Presbytery Gathering   30
(James B. Parks)

Section II: Preaching in a Season of Unrest

Alongside: Takin' It to the Streets   35
(Daris S. Bultena)

Wilderness Church   42
(Andrew Foster Connors)

Before and After   48
(Andrew J. Gathman)

Love in the Season of Riots: Baltimore 2015 (Christa Fuller Burns)	56
The Fields of Mondawmin (Kenneth E. Kovacs)	61
Just Sad (Alison Halsey)	67
Life Together: Branches of the Vine (John V. Carlson)	72
Things That Defile (Stephen R. Melton)	76
Why Are You Afraid? (Tanya Denley)	83
Five Smooth Stones (Jeanne E. Gay)	91
A Peculiar Instinct (Robert Hoch)	98
A Stronghold in Times of Trouble (Roger Scott Powers)	107
Things that Make for Peace (Brandon Frick)	116

Section III: Looking to the Future

Let the Boys Live! 127
      (Keith O. Paige)

Before It's Too Late 133
      (Ronnie A. Hankins)

Black Lives Matter 142
      (Tim Stern)

Hunting for the Kingdom ... on the Other Side? 150
      (Deborah McEachran)

Remember Who You Are 156
      (James B. Parks)

Jesus Wept 167
      (Tanya Wade)

From Hope to Wholeness 175
      (Mary D. Gaut)

Foreword

In April 2015, the long-smoldering embers of racial tension in Baltimore City erupted into flames and riots at a level unseen in 50 years. The riots were sparked by the death of Freddie Gray, a 25-year-old man who was arrested by the Baltimore Police Department for possessing what the police alleged was an illegal switchblade. While being transported in a police van, Gray was injured, fell into a coma, and was taken to a trauma center where he later died.

The riots served as a long-needed wake-up call for a community that had ignored for decades the systematic racism that thwarted and neglected the needs and aspirations of its African American brothers and sisters.

Within days of the riots, the Presbytery of Baltimore began mobilizing to be used by God to help foster healing and real change in the city. While many of our teaching and ruling elders were involved in various organizations and activities to combat racism, poverty and class discrimination, the Presbytery had not acted in a unified manner to address these issues.

Led by an *ad hoc* committee of teaching and ruling elders, the Presbytery issued a call for the issues of race, class and poverty to be addressed in church services, Christian education classes and in sermons. The Presbytery voted to focus its meetings for an entire year on these three issues.

As a Presbytery, we recognize that we, too, have failed to live up to Christ's command to love our neighbors as ourselves (Mark 12:33). We have come a long way toward putting these issues at the center of our mission, but we know we still have many miles to go.

This collection of sermons, prayers and liturgies by members of our Presbytery is just a sample of the work we are doing. We hope they will inspire the readers to examine these issues and join us in a prophetic witness as we journey with hope toward wholeness and toward fulfilling God's command to "let justice *roll down like waters* and righteousness *like an ever-flowing stream*" (Amos 5:24).

The Editors:

Rev. John V. Carlson
Rev. Mary D. Gaut
Rev. Jeanne E. Gay
Ruling Elder James B. Parks

Concerning the Organization of this Volume

This book is arranged in three sections. Section I is a collection of prayers and other responses to the unrest in Baltimore of 2015, mostly written and delivered around April 27-28, at the height of the uprising. Two of the offerings were utilized during a Presbytery-sponsored prayer vigil that week.

Section II is comprised partly of sermons preached on several Sundays at the end of April and the beginning of May, 2015, and then several more sermons preached in June, following the shootings at the Emanuel African Methodist Episcopal Church in Charleston, South Carolina.

Section III includes sermons that seem to be turning an eye to the future: two from the period of the unrest, and then several more from around the time of Dr. King's birthday in January, 2016, and one from that spring, as the one-year anniversary of the unrest approached. The final offering was delivered at an Interfaith Prayer Service commemorating the anniversary of the uprising.

Because many of the preachers in the Presbytery of Baltimore follow the Revised Common Lectionary, the sermons are grouped within each section according the Scripture text that was used. The passage is printed before each cluster of sermons, rather than repeating it for each offering, utilizing the New Revised Standard Edition of the Bible, copyright 1989 by the Division of Christian Education of the National Council of the Churches of Christ in the United States of America.

The Editors

SECTION I:
A Response of Prayer

Loving My Neighbor for Christ:
A Call to Prayer

Tanya S. Wade

> You did not choose me but I chose you. And I appointed you to go and bear fruit, fruit that will last, so that the Father will give you whatever you ask him in my name. I am giving you these commands so that you may love one another. John 15:16-17

By now, we are all aware of the unrest and state of emergency in our beloved city of Baltimore. Even with the violence there is a clear purpose and united concern for justice, transparency, and support for Freddie Gray's family. Beyond the national news there is a large group of citizens including clergy who are demonstrating and protesting in an intentional peaceful manner.

I stood among one such demonstration last night which was a movement for peace in our streets, justice and transparency. This was a movement filled with prayer as clergy, believers, and citizens walked the streets. We witnessed the power of God as people of different backgrounds and points of view came together as one. Upon returning to the church, gang members met us. They were riding in and standing on top of a black SUV shouting out their pain and requirement for justice.

I turned to see ... one block up the street ... a vehicle had been set on fire by some other group. My husband, Anthony, and I were there. Standing amid the storm.

Watching it unfold before us. Instead of running we stood and prayed. We prayed with clergy, citizens and gang members. People of God began to pull the gang members from the vehicle. We hugged them, we prayed with them and we cried together for all of our pain.

Together, all of us entered New Shiloh Baptist Church and began to talk. We found that there are many sides to this story. The gang members were actually members from several gangs in the community. They came together as "BROTHERS" to help stop the violence. They formed lines in front of stores owned by African Americans and Muslims. They encouraged those who had chosen the path of violence to now show restraint. They also reported that while they were helping to stop the violence the police bombed them with tear gas.

This is a moment when we need to hear every story. This is a moment which, with God's help, we can transform into a better and stronger community.

Tonight the clergy and others who are concerned will meet at New Shiloh Baptist Church located at 2100 N. Monroe Street at 6:00 p.m. This affects all of us and our presence is needed. I am asking that if you cannot join us … please pray with us from wherever you are. Pray for the peace of Christ to touch every heart … pray for justice, pray for transparency, pray for the Gray family, pray for all people who have been profiled/victimized/killed, pray for people who chose violence (citizens and police), and pray that the power and presence of God shall reside upon all of us.

God's people, this is a call to not only to believe but to put into action the promises of God: "You did not choose me, but I chose you and appointed you so that you might go and bear fruit—fruit that will last—and so that whatever you ask in my name the Father will give you. This is my command: Love each other." (John 15:16-17) This is a call to PRAYER and PRESENCE!!!!

The Rev. Tanya Wade is Pastor at Grace Presbyterian Church, a congregation of 182 in northwest Baltimore City. She was the first African American woman to be ordained in Baltimore Presbytery.

A Litany for the City

Carrie Finch-Burriss

For all who are gathered here today, who love and serve your city Lord—
Let there be justice; let there be peace.

For those who have been hurt, for those who have been chased, for those who have suffered—
Let there be justice; let there be peace.

For the family and friends of Freddie Gray—
Let there be justice; let there be peace.

For those who serve and protect, for those who are willing to sacrifice their lives—
Let there be justice; let there be peace.

For the owners of the businesses looted and destroyed—
Let there be justice; let there be peace.

For those whose voices have been silenced for too long—
Let there be justice; let there be peace.

For those who stand up for and work for justice and peace.
Let there be justice; let there be peace.

For those who are afraid, who long for safety—
Let there be justice; let there be peace.

For Sandtown, for Winchester, for Harlem Park—
Let there be justice; let there be peace.

For those who are unemployed, for those who are hungry and poor—
Let there be justice; let there be peace.

For our schools, for our children, for our future—
> **Let there be justice; let there be peace.**

For this great city of Baltimore—
> **Let there be justice; let there be peace.**

The Rev. Carrie Finch-Burriss serves as Pastor of Kenwood Presbyterian Church, a congregation of about 120 in Baltimore. This litany was part of the Flames for Peace and Justice Prayer Vigil held by the presbytery on Friday, May 1, 2015.

Prayer for Justice

James B. Parks

Dear God,

You command us in the book of Isaiah to "Learn to do good; seek justice, correct oppression; bring justice to the fatherless, plead the widow's cause." Today, Lord, we confess that instead of following your word, we have allowed our greed and fear of strangers to create a world where the few are living very large at the expense of the many. Today, dear Lord, on the streets of Baltimore and on streets across this land, people are crying out for justice, for an end to decades of living in the strait jackets of poverty, injustice and oppression.

Dear Lord, we cry out for justice for Freddie Gray and all people who have been mistreated by the enforcers of our-human-made laws. We recognize, Lord, that the large majority of those who patrol our streets are good men and women who care about justice, but there are some who do not. We pray today for the souls of the Baltimore police, the state's attorney's office, the courts, the governor, the legislature, the mayor and the City Council, that they may become the true instruments of justice that you call them to be.

We pray for our souls as well. Help us to become fulltime, everyday outlets for your love and justice. Help us to see your light in all people. We cry out, dear God, for justice for those who felt the only way to have their voices heard is through violence. As your people, Lord, we condemn all violence, but as a compassionate people we understand the anger and desperation that led to the violence. We pray for the souls of the families who are trapped in Baltimore's poor communities, some of the poorest in the country, where low tax revenue means less money for schools, which means poor education, which leads to few or no good jobs, which leads to alternative and often illegal ways to put food on the table, which leads to prison, which leads to broken homes, which begins the cycle of desperation all over again. So today, dear God, we cry out for justice to roll down like a mighty stream. We cry out Lord, for justice! Hear our cry!

Please, now dear Lord, hear our prayers as individually we now name aloud or silently in our hearts those for whom we seek justice:

SILENT PRAYER

These things we ask in the name of Jesus. And all God's people said, Amen.

Ruling Elder James B. Parks served as Moderator of the Presbytery of Baltimore during 2015-16, and is a member of Hunting Ridge Presbyterian Church. This prayer was part of the Flames for Peace and Justice Prayer Vigil held by the presbytery on Friday, May 1, 2015.

A Prayer of Confession for the City of Baltimore

Ronnie A. Hankins

Precious and Mighty God, we recognize you as the as the Alpha and the Omega, the beginning and the end.

Yet along our daily journey between the beginning and the end of each and every day, we as a people still somehow fail to acknowledge the needs of those who struggle and suffer along with us during this journey and as a result… We greatly ignore the economic, social and institutional inequalities that polarize people according to race, gender, and economic class, all of which keep our communities strongly at odds with one another.

And we ask, why are the people so angry?

Have Mercy upon us O Lord.

We often ignore the many Freddie Grays within our communities and their families who make their living by living on the edge, barely able to survive within this callous, dog-eat-dog society which repeated tells an impoverished, struggling people walking without boots, to just pull themselves up by their boot-straps.

And we ask, why are the people so angry?

Have Mercy upon us O Lord.

We gruff at the ever growing number of cardboard signs held beneath of the faces of the homeless deemed by society to be unwanted outcasts and misfits, written off as being simply too lazy to go out and find work And as we close the eyes of our hearts as we drive past them, their eyes open every day to a dream which has now become a living nightmare.

And we ask why are the people so angry?

Have Mercy upon us O Lord.

We shake our heads at the struggle and inability of many citizens of color to gain any traction beyond the socio-economic impedance brought on by past centuries of enslavement and Jim-Crowism, resulting in generations of families struggling to obtain just a small piece of the American dream. They watch painfully and resentfully, as other foreign groups come into their poor neighbors and are easily given access to resources enabling their dreams to come true, prospering and profiting in the neighborhoods of those who can't seem to get ahead.

And we ask, why are the people so angry?

Have Mercy upon us O Lord.

We watch the poor and the impoverished continue in their institutionalized oppression as conservative political ideologies seek to dismantle and take away social resources and stepping stones designed to lend assistance to the poor and give some opportunity of advancement to the disadvantaged and disenfranchised, all under the hypocritical chicanery of attempting to sound charitable, while not being charitable at all. We stand by and watch as wealthy politicians repeatedly give themselves pay raises while in subterfuge, vote against any sort of increase in minimum or living wages for the poor, all under the guise of fiscal conservatism.

And we ask, why are the people so angry?

Have Mercy upon us O Lord.

Then … as the people scream out in frustration and anger, as stores are looted—their windows shattered by the tossing of gasoline filled bottles, and the sounds of breaking glass is heard from burning police cruisers are they are set ablaze—black smoke billows into the skies as hopeless angry citizens stare down into the faces of city police officers standing arm to arm in riot gear. … We shake our heads in confusion asking the question *What is wrong with those people and why are they doing this to our city? Those people…*

And we ask why are the people so angry?

Have Mercy upon us O Lord.

A wise man once said the only thing necessary for unintended catastrophic consequences, is for good people to do nothing. Help us O Lord to act out of a spirit of Christian love and compassion, before the glass starts to break and the fires begin to burn.

Help us O Lord.

Help us too, O God, to be a people of **conscience**, remembering the words of Dr. Martin Luther King who reminded us that *Cowardice asks the question—is it safe? Expediency asks the question—is it politic? Vanity asks the question—is it popular? But conscience asks the question—is it right?*

Have Mercy upon us O Lord.

Help us too, O God, ponder the words of a convicted felon who said: Don't judge me for the choices I made when you don't know the options I had to choose from.

Have Mercy upon us O Lord.

Help us too, O God, remember and reflect upon the words of James Baldwin who said *Ignorance, allied with power, is the most ferocious enemy justice can have.*

Have Mercy upon us O Lord.

Help us O God to recognize that even a small spark of justice ignites a blaze of joy and happiness amongst God's creation, while cruel injustices having gone ignored and smothered, suffocate us all with the black smoke of unrighteousness.

Have Mercy upon us O Lord.

For those of us who might question the relevancy or significance of someone arrested by the police who dies while in their custody, help us O God to remember the story of a convicted thief on the cross who had the audacity to trust in the Lord Jesus Christ despite their accompanying death sentences, thus prompting Christ to put his own death on pause for just a moment in order to share Paradise with someone deemed by the world to be a societal catastrophe, but deemed by Christ to be a pearl of great price.

Let us never forget your grace and mercy O Lord.

We lift up all of those here in Baltimore deemed societally catastrophic by some, yet precious in the sight of God, whose soiled faces, worn bodies and bootless feet bear the scars and wounds of their long and painful journey.

We lift the people up to you in prayer O Lord.

Leader: Help us O God as a people and a police force to live peacefully and support one another. Let the unnecessary killing amongst people of color stop, not just here in Baltimore, but throughout our nation. Let there be justice in the city of Baltimore and let it roll on like a river, and righteousness like an ever-flowing stream. Let the targeting of people of color with extreme prejudicial violence by those sworn to uphold the peace come to an immediate cease. And help us O Lord as a city to not just articulate the important phrase Black Lives Matter, but to also live it by not killing our own people.

Help us O Lord.

Forgive us as a city for not caring enough for one another as we should. Help us to be not just hearers of your Word, but also doers of your Word. Help us O God to shatter the glass walls and ceilings of hate and ignorance, rather than shatter glass windows of homes and businesses within our communities through violence and anger generated out of callous insensitivity, never-ending injustice and a sense of hopelessness and despair. Let us as a city find a new and living hope through the resurrection of Jesus Christ that will result in a profound love and respect for one another, as well as a genuine concern for the safety and well-being of every citizen.

We lift the people of Baltimore up to you in prayer O Lord!

In the Holy and Precious name of Jesus Christ we pray.

Amen

> **The Rev. Ronnie Hankins**, a former Moderator of the Presbytery of Baltimore, is Pastor at Trinity Presbyterian Church, a congregation of 109 members located in Baltimore, very near to where much of the uprising of April 2015 unfolded.

Two Facets of Justice

Renee Mackey

I. Justice Cries

She lurks behind the corner
Terrified
I wonder if it's safe?

He glances over each shoulder
Suspicious
I wonder why that car is following me?

The children run on the playground
Searching
I wonder if I'll step on a protruding needle?

The feet of the worker step across the beam
Doubtful
I wonder if my insurance will cover me if I fall?

The fingers on the keyboard type in a message
Fearful
I wonder if a bully will respond?

The family huddles against the wind seeking shelter
Worried
I wonder if I'll have food tonight?

Are these my only responses? Where is God?
Whatever happened to hopes and dreams?
Did they vanish behind closed doors?

II. Justice Moves

She boldly strolls around the block
Calm
I know I will not be assaulted

He concentrates on the street ahead
Relaxed
I know I won't hear any gun shots

Children skip and dash in and out
Laughing
I know no danger lurks beneath my feet

The worker walks the length of the beam
Confident
I know my claim will be honored

The screen lights up with a text message
Self-assured
I know I won't have to delete any racial slurs

The homeless family smiles to an outstretched hand
Secure
I know my needs will be met

Positive approaches to life; God's love in action
Dreams transformed into reality
People creating safe spaces for all to enter

Rev. Renee Mackey, a former moderator of the Presbytery of Baltimore, serves as Pastor of the 80-member Covenant Presbyterian Church, Hagerstown, MD, about 75 miles west of the city of Baltimore.

Personal Note: Baltimore Presbytery Gathering

James B. Parks

On a personal note, I've heard that some members of our Presbytery think all this talk about race, poverty and class only shows our continued bias for Baltimore and that it doesn't relate to or affect them. That frankly is not true. The issues of race, poverty and class exist in every pocket of this Presbytery whether we choose to admit it or not. God did not create the riots, but God is calling us to use the events of April to spread His love and justice and to reconcile the different communities where His children live. Without getting into a complicated theological discussion, I simply ask you to think of the reasons why you would enthusiastically give money, time and energy to support missions for people in need on the other side of the world and not to help those who live next door.

The reality is that times are hard everywhere, both inside and outside Baltimore. A recent federal government report shows that rural areas in Maryland have higher unemployment rates, lower high school graduation rates, and higher poverty rates than urban areas. And anyone who lives there can tell you that the problems of the city are spreading to other towns like Annapolis, Columbia and Hagerstown, which are becoming urban centers themselves, having to cope with poverty, drugs, poor housing and crime.

A mother grieves over the death of her child whether he dies from exhaustion and exposure at the Hungary-Serbia border or from a gunshot in West Baltimore. A child with no food is just as hungry in Cumberland as he is in Baltimore. A father whose child is on drugs is just as much at wits' end whether he lives in Columbia or East Baltimore. A family that can't pay the rent suffers just as much from being shut out in the cold whether it's in Fallston, Frederick or South Baltimore. We are all in this together, and God doesn't allow us to pick and choose which of Her children to whom we show love.

Let us not forget the words of our Lord Jesus in Matthew 25:37-40:

> Then the righteous will answer him, Lord when was it that we saw you hungry and gave you food, or thirsty and gave you something to drink? And when was it that we saw you naked and gave you clothing? And when was it that we saw you sick or in prison and visited you? And the King will answer and say to them, 'Truly I tell you, just as you did it to one of the least of these who are members of my family, you did it to me."

God is truly working in our presbytery. I thank God for giving us the opportunity to serve in such a special cause.

Ruling Elder James B. Parks was Moderator of the Presbytery of Baltimore during 2015-16, and is a member of Hunting Ridge Presbyterian Church. These remarks were delivered to the 868th Gathering of the Presbytery of Baltimore, September 17, 2015.

SECTION II:
Preaching in a Season of Unrest

Alongside: Takin' It to the Streets

Daris S. Bultena

Then an angel of the Lord said to Philip, "Get up and go toward the south to the road that goes down from Jerusalem to Gaza." (This is a wilderness road.) So he got up and went. Now there was an Ethiopian eunuch, a court official of the Candace, queen of the Ethiopians, in charge of her entire treasury. He had come to Jerusalem to worship and was returning home; seated in his chariot, he was reading the prophet Isaiah. Then the Spirit said to Philip, "Go over to this chariot and join it." So Philip ran up to it and heard him reading the prophet Isaiah. He asked, "Do you understand what you are reading?" He replied, "How can I, unless someone guides me?" And he invited Philip to get in and sit beside him.

Now the passage of the scripture that he was reading was this:
"Like a sheep he was led to the slaughter,
    and like a lamb silent before its shearer,
        so he does not open his mouth.
In his humiliation justice was denied him.
        Who can describe his generation?
        For his life is taken away from the earth."

The eunuch asked Philip, "About whom, may I ask you, does the prophet say this, about himself or about someone else?" Then Philip began to speak, and starting with this scripture, he proclaimed to him the good news about Jesus. As they were going along the road, they came to some water; and the eunuch said, "Look, here is water! What is to prevent me from being baptized?" [And Phillip said, "If you believe with all your heart, you may." And he replied, "I believe that Jesus Christ is the Son of God."] He commanded the chariot to stop, and both of them, Philip and the eunuch, went down into the water, and Philip baptized him. When they came up out of the water, the Spirit of the Lord snatched Philip away; the eunuch saw him no more, and went on his way rejoicing. But Philip found himself at Azotus, and as he was passing through the region, he proclaimed the good news to all the towns until he came to Caesarea. Acts 8:26-40

I have this orange tree. The tree lives outside all summer long and into the fall. Once it starts to get cold, I bring it in the house. It does not do well in the house. It doesn't die, but it loses its leaves.

The other day I moved the thing outside. It was heavy. Very heavy, and way heavier than one would think a leafless tree should be.

It has been outside now for six days. I'm no longer passing by the leafless branches in my house.

*

As I was recovering from carrying that heavy thing outside, I sat down. It was in my recovery period that I saw the breaking news come on the television. School had let out, and West Baltimore began to come apart. I heard what I thought not possible—that the young people outnumbered the police.

Like so many of us, I could not leave my chair. I just kept watching as one event unfolded into the next event.

From rock throwing to burning buildings, and from looting to unhinged behavior—it was protest and police lines and then what felt more like crazy and crisis than anything else.

*

What do we do when such things happen? Do we watch in horror? We did. Do we weep in sadness? Yes. While we live "out here" some 13 miles away, it is **our** city. When we travel around the country or world and someone asks, "Where are you from?" We say, "Baltimore." All our surrounding communities are part of this city of ours. We are all from Baltimore.

So what do we Baltimoreans do when such things happen? When there is rioting and disruption and injustice or corruption—just what do we do? What do we do as things get more frayed? What do we do when those we are supposed to trust don't seem so trustworthy? What do we do as our racial divisions widen and people separate from one another?

What **we** do—what we Christians do—we look to the scriptures. We come together, we pray, and we pour it out before God. We look to the scriptures and we ask—"Where is God in all this" and "Where do we fit in this to try and make sense of it all."

*

There in the book of Acts is this story in Chapter 8. It is the story of Philip and the Ethiopian. It is the action in the story. There are three players in this story. There is Philip, there is the Ethiopian, and there is the Spirit of God. To read this story as only being about Philip and the Ethiopian is to miss the story. God is a central player in the story and is active.

*

It is where the story begins to shape our reality this week as Baltimoreans. Let us be clear that our story is not only a story about ones seeking justice and protestors and police and rioters and those trying to stop the rioting. There is another player in our story—a player that seems unseen to many—but a player that is in there. God. God is in all this.

That is the good news of the story. Both now and in the book of Acts. God is in this.

As the story in Acts begins, it says: "Then an angel of the Lord said to Philip, "Get up and go."

Now Philip was headed the other way when he receives this instruction. "Get up and go." It is it is the presence of God that reached out and laid claim to Philip and said, "Here is what I want you to do."

God called Philip into active service. Philip, as a follower of Christ, was to both be listening for that call and be receptive to it. Philip was to be that vessel through which the presence of God could move.

Such is how God works for us who are his followers of Christ. There is within us this voice—call it an angel, call it the Spirit, call it the presence of God. There is that voice within us that calls us up into service.

Our job is to be responsive to that voice and step up and move forward even when it goes the opposite direction of what our natural inclination is to go. That voice is not an audible "You do this now" voice—it is that inner prompting. That gut feeling. That nudge—gentle sometimes and at other times an all-out push. That friend or that colleague. That voice we hear as we gather together—the voice of each other. **That** is the God-breathed, Spirit voice prompting us to answer the claim of God on our life.

God had a purpose for Philip that day. "Get up and go."

God has a purpose for us today. "Get up and go." Our job is not to let events unfold and watch them on television. Our job is to be actively up and going. We are to be up and going with prayer. We are to be up and going figuring out how it is we help to shift the world to be a more just, more loving, and more peaceful place for ALL God's children to dwell.

"Get up and go."

*

And Philip went. When we heed those promptings we end up in the right place and are able to discern even further what the call of God is on our lives. Philip did not just go—he had specific instructions that involved physical effort on his part.

Find the chariot. Go over to the chariot. Join it. So Philip goes. Philip runs alongside it. Philip climbs onboard.

It is that image of Philip running alongside the chariot. That image is the image of the call of the Christian life. We are to be running alongside those who are on the way. We are to be alongside those who are in the street and even those who have taken to the streets.

To be alongside is to be in relationship. To be alongside is to acknowledge that the other is worthwhile. To lay claim to the gospel truth that all people are God's people and **all** are God's own children.

That Ethiopian would have not been included at other points in the life of the temple and worship. Did Philip see a barrier there? No, because God did not. God saw that Ethiopian as God's own and sent Philip to him.

It is what we must see and understand as we look to our own streets. **All**—in here and out there—are included. We are to come alongside. Our Christ runs alongside those who have taken to the streets.

Our Christ has always been the advocate for justice and peace. That is who we are to be and it is how we live this life. Will we differ on how to do that? Of course we will. But those differences should not diminish us but call us to be in conversation and in relationship. As we live out those relationships and have those conversations the walls between us tumble down.

Alongside. Not alone. Our momentum is about being alongside. And like Philip that takes physical effort on our part. We invest ourselves when we go alongside others and discover that we have more in common than we have differences.

*

Philip comes alongside that Ethiopian, and then he guides him.

Philip asks him, "Do you understand what you are reading?" And the Ethiopian replies, "How can I, unless someone guides me?" Philip guides him; Philip shows him Christ.

Be Philip. Show them Christ. His way is the way. It is the way that puts love first. It is the way that connects others to God. It is the way that shows we are the branches of his vine. From Christ flows that life which makes the way for us.

Love. Peace. Mercy. Hope. Justice. Grace. Love. And more love. That is what it is all about. Take it to the streets of our Baltimore ... that is the sign we will wave in the crowd. It is what we will wear. Love. Peace. Mercy. Hope. Justice. Grace. Love. And more love.

It is what we give ... it is how we guide one another.

*

It was six days ago that so much happened on our streets. It was also six days ago I lugged that leafless tree outside. But **today**, that leafless tree has sprouted leaves and many have grown. There is this new life that is bursting forth.

That is our city ... there can be this new life that grows out of all this. And we are those new leaves that are sprouting. As we come alongside others ... as we step up and step out ... as we get up and get going. We are those new leaves that are sprouting.

Amen.

The Rev. Daris Bultena serves as Pastor of Good Shepherd Presbyterian Church a congregation of 227 in Joppatowne, MD, about 20 miles northeast of Baltimore in Harford County. Daris is a past moderator of the presbytery.

Wilderness Church

Andrew Foster Connors

It's customary for a church to give a gift at baptism. We often give books. Idlewild Church where I served in Memphis gives a tree to plant. Another church gives out handmade baby quilts. But reading Acts I think baptism ought to come with a pair of running shoes. The amount of walking involved seems extensive. You get baptized into the faith of Jesus, and immediately the Spirit is zinging you off on some unexpected assignment. "Get up and go," the Spirit tells Philip and he's off to the road that leads to Gaza, a distance of some sixty miles from Jerusalem where, apparently, God needs the gospel proclaimed immediately. He starts out, but soon learns that Gaza is not the destination. The ministry happens on the way, in an encounter that was completed unexpected for Philip.

Following Jesus means a lot of uncertainty for the apostles in Acts. Sometimes proclaiming the Gospel takes the disciples head to head with the powers that be. Sometimes it brings them to people who want to be healed. Sometimes it carries them to people who want to be taught. Sometimes it zooms them to people who need to be listened to. The Spirit of God is always pushing disciples out into the world into new and unusual circumstances, equipped only with the story of Jesus and the ministry that usually seems to happen on the way to somewhere else.

We don't know how Philip felt about these sudden assignments. The text reports only his obedience. We don't know whether he was reluctant, or tired, or angry, or irritated or glad to go. But we do know that Philip's particular assignment was a risky one. He was told to travel the wilderness road. The wilderness road is not the kind of road you want to travel. Full of uncertainty, danger, scarcity. It's the wilderness that everybody loathes. The place where the Israelites cry out to God for food and water. The place where John the Baptist announces the urgency of repentance. The wilderness road is not the road that you want to travel.

It's certainly not the road any of us would have chosen this week as youth staged a pitched battle with police in the streets, malls and grocery stories were looted, cars smashed, and a senior center was burned to the ground. Walking the streets on Tuesday I certainly felt the sadness and anger. I listened to people in Sandtown shaking their heads wondering how they were going to eat when the grocery store was empty from the looting; how they were going to get their medicines when the CVS had burned. Like many of you I had phone calls from people outside the state watching CNN portray our city as if every single corner was under siege. Even with all that we know about the more than justified anger in the streets, the injustices leveled against whole communities that do not feel they have a stake in the success of the city, the wilderness the whole city found itself in was not the path that most people in Baltimore would have chosen.

Nobody chooses the wilderness road if they can take another way. The wilderness road is full of uncertainty, danger, and scarcity. Given a choice, nobody takes the wilderness road.

And yet the biblical story reports that wilderness is the place where faith is most readily found. When you have nothing, you turn to God quickly for support.

The rabbis taught that the Israelites had to wander in the desert for forty years, not because Moses was bad at directions, but because it took that long for them to trust in God completely. The wilderness road is not the road you want to travel and yet it is the road that leads to faith. Wilderness and promise are intertwined. Death and resurrection are interconnected. Dying and rising are inextricable from each other.

I saw it on Tuesday morning when we showed up at the triangle in Sandtown, across from St. Peter Claver Church. Hundreds of people from all over the city showed up with gloves and rakes and trash bags to clean up. You could feel the hope rising up from an inexplicable place.

I heard it at 11 AM when I ferried one of the neighborhood leaders in Sandtown to a closed-door session with the Governor. Rather than hearing from Shabazz or Sharpton or one of the many celebrity interpreters of what residents in Sandtown want, the Sandtown leader herself spoke directly to the Governor. And he listened.

I saw it at 2:00 in our assembly room when BUILD pastors, and Sandtown leaders, and concerned citizens— many from our church—listened to one another identify the needs and strategize about a response. Nobody would have chosen the destruction of our city if there had been another path, but there we all were—Christians, Jews, neighbors from Sandtown and Bolton Hill, students and concerned citizens—all together strategizing about how to make sure everyone got their bread that day.

I saw it again at 5:30 that afternoon when many of you along with people from Corpus Christi and Memorial Episcopal and First and Franklin and neighbors gathered to pray and sing. Nobody would have chosen the occasion for that worship service, and yet prayer and song and loving your neighbor as yourself has never felt more important than it did that night.

And I saw it in the fellowship hall of St. Peter Claver Church that night where more than 150 people gathered sharing food and stories. I listened to neighbors tired of the violence not just on Monday but for decades. Tired of police brutality not just with Freddie Gray, but for decades. Tired of unemployment, and hardship. Tired of cameras and people speaking for them without asking them about their own hopes and goals and concerns.

The wilderness is a tricky place. It's not the place of ease and comfort, but it is the place where the purpose of your life is clarified. It's not the place of joy and thanksgiving, but it often leads to both. It's not the place you would choose to be, but you're almost always guaranteed to meet God there.

And maybe that's one of the lessons our church can relearn this week. It's the wilderness times—those times that no one would choose for ourselves—that define our faith. It's the wilderness times where God can most readily be found. The wilderness time of clergy and members of this church arrested in 1963 to force the integration of a park. Nobody knew how many members the church might lose, but God met them on the way and the time defined our faith. The wilderness time of this congregation that almost closed in the late '70s, and a small faithful remnant uncertain of everything except their commitment to ministry in the city. God met them on the way, and that time defined our faith. The wilderness of debates over LGBT inclusion that tore at the fabric of the church and the humanity of those seeking only to be a part of the family of God. God met you on the way, and that time defined our faith.

It's those wilderness times that define our faith. Those wilderness roads we travel without any kind of certainty of the destination or even the assignment. Those wilderness roads where ministry happens on the way. It's those wilderness times that define our faith, and I can't help but believe that we have entered one of those times again when the curtain has been pulled back on the two Baltimores that we've all come to know, and we have to decide whether to answer the Spirit's call another time with all the uncertainty that following Jesus entails; knowing that sometimes proclaiming the Gospel takes disciples head to head with the powers that be. Sometimes it brings them to people who want to be healed. Sometimes it carries them to people who want to be taught. Sometimes it zooms them to people who need to be listened to. The Spirit of God is always pushing disciples out into the world into new and unusual circumstances, equipped only with the story of Jesus and the ministry that usually seems to happen on the way to somewhere else.

Only a few things were required of Philip that day he met the African official. He had to listen, share the good news, and accept this man as his brother in the faith. He had to listen to the person God had put before him. He had to share the good news of Christ's resurrection in the context of crucifixion. And he had to accept the miraculous truth that the church God is building includes everyone who wants to be a part of it.

In Sandtown on Tuesday night after some time around tables, I ended up outside listening to two mothers and a grandmother reflecting on the events of the week. We ate pizza leaning over the bed of their pickup truck. They told me how hard it was to sleep with the helicopters circling all night, the loudspeaker commanding people to go inside or be arrested. They shared their anxieties—where to find food with no grocery store. Where to get blood pressure medication with no CVS and buses still not running. The conversation quickly turned in a more hopeful direction. People are resilient, and when you're used to living day to day maybe it's easier to adapt in a crisis. One of the women asked me to pray with them and we did.

To anyone who might have noticed us, I'm sure we looked like an odd church. The body of Christ shared in pizza on the communion table of a pickup truck. People brought together across short distances that seem like chasms in this city where we live. But if you know the Spirit, it could be the seeds of the next great assignment for the church, equipped with little more than food and water and a gospel story that promises to upend all of our present arrangements and reorganize them around a table where life is shared and wilderness begins to look like home.

The Rev. Andrew Foster Connors serves as Pastor of Brown Memorial Presbyterian Church, a 305-member church in the Bolton Hill section of Baltimore, just a few miles from the center of the unrest.

Before and After

Andrew J. Gathman

Beloved, let us love one another, because love is from God; everyone who loves is born of God and knows God. Whoever does not love does not know God, for God is love. God's love was revealed among us in this way: God sent his only Son into the world so that we might live through him. In this is love, not that we loved God but that he loved us and sent his Son to be the atoning sacrifice for our sins. Beloved, since God loved us so much, we also ought to love one another. No one has ever seen God; if we love one another, God lives in us, and his love is perfected in us.

By this we know that we abide in him and he in us, because he has given us of his Spirit. And we have seen and do testify that the Father has sent his Son as the Savior of the world. God abides in those who confess that Jesus is the Son of God, and they abide in God. So we have known and believe the love that God has for us.

God is love, and those who abide in love abide in God, and God abides in them. Love has been perfected among us in this: that we may have boldness on the day of judgment, because as he is, so are we in this world. There is no fear in love, but perfect love casts out fear; for fear has to do with punishment, and whoever fears has not reached perfection in love. We love because he first loved us. Those who say, "I love God," and hate their brothers or sisters, are liars; for those who do not love a brother or sister whom they have seen, cannot love God whom they have not seen. The commandment we have from him is this: those who love God must love their brothers and sisters also.   1 John 4:7-21

Well, it's been quite a week, hasn't it? Quite a before and after. Before the week began, it was more or less business as usual in Baltimore. After, it is anything but. Before the week began, people could get around downtown freely, the Orioles were playing to a packed house, Harbor Place was bustling, and people were talking mostly about the weather. But after, well, there's lots to talk about, isn't there? Massive protests and demonstrations almost every day, businesses have been looted and burned, a state of emergency was been declared, and a citywide curfew is still in effect.

For me, the most haunting of the before and after pictures is of a corner store in the heart of Northwest. After being looted, it was set on fire, destroying everything inside. If that's not bad enough, the adjacent rowhouse also caught fire, which housed Portia Lawson and her 7-year-old son KhaiLee, who has cerebral palsy. They lost everything, including the wheelchair that KhaiLee needs to get around. What did they do to be the victims of such rage? She was doing everything right—taking responsibility for her family in a challenging situation, doing what she could to make ends meet, sharing such love as she could in the place that she called home. And now it's gone, taken away in a frenzy of senseless violence.

It's a tragic story, one of many such stories in Baltimore City right now. There are many ways to characterize this week's before and after, but one way would be to say simply that it has been a graphic depiction of what happens when the fears and hatreds that have plagued the human race for time untold bubble to the surface and finally erupt. Residents in fear of police, black in fear of white—and white of black. Rich in fear of poor. Slice it how you will, but these fears of those who are different steal into our souls and petrify our hearts; they harden into hatreds that, though unspoken, become a disease that runs through every corner of society.

Perhaps the events of this week are so disturbing because they have shattered the illusion that we are immune to the consequences of our fears and hatreds—that here in Baltimore they are somehow contained and safe, that we're insulated or isolated from them actually harming us. Sure, it might happen in other countries, or in other cities, but we—surely we are not so bad. But in defiance of our denial, what we have seen this week is as clear a picture as we can get of what happens when we allow our fears and hatreds to fester—it is a picture of the hell that awaits us if we allow them to remain.

And we ourselves are complicit in it. Oh, sure, we may not have been involved in any of these incidents directly. We may not have beaten the prisoner, or looted the shops, or stoked the fires of racial hatred with incendiary remarks, but we have sat comfortably by while thousands live in squalor not 20 miles from our door; we have enjoyed the benefits of a system that works largely to our favor giving little thought to those for whom the system is a broken mess; we have indulged in thinking we have what we have by nothing more than the sweat of our brow and the ingenuity of our minds, looking down on those who fail to pick themselves up as if they are morally defective because of it. We are complicit if for no other reason than we are part of the same city, the same human family that is entangled in the same sins, the same fears, the same hatreds we've seen erupting on our TV screens this week.

To those who would be unmoved by what we have seen this week—by the plight of neighbors who have watched their livelihoods destroyed, by the desperation of the protestors in their demands for justice, by the systemic evils the week's violence has revealed, to those who would be witness to such things and remain unaffected, John's letter today contains some harsh words: "Those who say, 'I love God,' and hate their brothers or sisters are liars; for those who do not love a brother or sister whom they have seen cannot love God whom they have not seen." Hatred, along with fear, which is the seed from which hatred grows, are incompatible with the love of God.

But to those who have been moved, I think the question that is on all of our minds is, what now? In all that has happened in the before and after, what could we possibly do, besides shake our head in disbelief or hang our head in shame or turn our head away in indifference? Tempting as it would be to ignore or forget, as difficult as it has been to watch Baltimore's before and after, John speaks in our passage today of another before and after, one that is equally dramatic—perhaps more so—one that gives us the power and the courage to respond in a moment like this.

"God's love was revealed among us in this way," John says in v. 9, "God sent his only son into the world so that we might live through him. In this is love, not that we loved God but that he loved us and sent his Son to be the atoning sacrifice for our sins."

You see, this condition of ours, our fear and hatred for one another, our deep-seated indifference to those outside our own group, this is not endemic to Baltimore, nor is it simply something that plagues this particular moment in world history, as we well know. What we saw in Baltimore this week was but a sad continuation of the story of humanity's inhumanity. It is the predictable outcome of the years of fear and hatred. Or, as humorist Jon Stewart put it, "these cyclical eruptions appear like tragedy cicadas, depressing in their similarity, predictability, and intractability."[1]

And it's not only the issues of race and class here in America. We see it all over the world, all throughout history, people dividing themselves from one another based on clan or class or creed. The Bible calls this condition sin, and tells us that these evils are not merely the product of poor upbringing or a faulty psychology but that they are part and parcel to the human condition—baked into the cake, so to speak, and passed down through the generations from the earliest days of the human race.

I mean, when the Bible's story of the first human brothers describes how the one killed the other in a fit of jealous rage, it's trying to tell you something profound about our origins. Friends, this is who we are. Sure, we love those who love us. But we fear those who do not. We are haters, oppressors, murderers, and war-makers.

And it is precisely to this warped, sinful, broken and hateful humanity that God sent his son. I mean, what good do we have that we could give him? What worship do we have that could please him? Not a thing. And yet God

---

[1] Stewart, Jon. "The Daily Show." Baltimore on Fire. CNN. 28 Apr. 2015. Television.

looked upon us in our misery and showed us love. A love so profound that it involved sending his Son to die, that we might live through him.

As the Gospels reveal, God's Son, Jesus Christ our Lord, suffered the same fate as countless other young men have suffered at the hands of the authorities: brutality, injustice, senseless death. And even then God did not withhold his love. You'd think God would have every reason to riot and rage over what happened to his son, but it was then that God demonstrated the full and profound power of his love. For, as John tells us, it was by that very sacrifice that our own sins—the same sins that put Jesus on that cross—were atoned for, and washed away.

In the depths of God's love for us, through Christ we were freed from the long curse of hatred and violence and death. What a stunning turn of events. What a dramatic before and after. Not that we loved God, but that God has loved us.

For the last few weeks, we have been looking in this Easter season at what it means to live in light of the resurrection. And if it is not clear yet, then it should be by now that we are profoundly transformed by Jesus' resurrection. We have been given a new lease on life. Change that—we have been given a new life. In Christ we have been so filled with the love of God that our old lives, the ones that were filled with fear and hatred, have been put to death—utterly destroyed. The old is gone, behold, all has become new. He has put a new heart in us, put a new spirit in us—the spirit of his holiness and mercy. God has done all of this in love, without our ever having deserved it.

But as John is keen to point out, the consequence of this fact is not simply warm feelings and a personal sense of well-being. No, the effects are dramatic and far-reaching, touching not only ourselves but everyone around us. "Beloved," John says in verse 11, "Since God loved us so much, we also ought to love one another." We know what we must do, because it is what God has done for us: not to pick up stones with those who rage against the system, not to wield the sword with those who fear an uprising, not to stand back and watch as the world burns. But to lay our weapons down, to lay our fears down, and to reach out in love.

To love not only those we find lovely or worthy or who we think will love us in return, but to see in the eyes of a stranger a human being who is loved by God. To engage deeply even with those who are different from us and to listen, and learn, and seek their good, to refuse to turn away out of anger or indifference. To treat all who come across our path as God treats us: as beloved children of God, who are cherished, and in spite of sin, have been redeemed.

Of course, we do not do this on our own, nor must we do it in a vacuum. "We love," John says in v. 19, "because he first loved us." That's the headline that makes all the difference in our lives. That's the big story that enables us to engage with all the smaller stories. That's the before-and-after that equips us to deal with Baltimore's and every other before and after. In our before, it was nothing but fear and hatred. But in the aftermath God's love, everything is changed. For we have become God's children, and we now find ourselves secure in his love, redeemed by his love, transformed through his love.

It is precisely because of this amazing before and after, having been caught up in the gracious and unfailing love of God, that we are now able to cultivate and demonstrate a love for others in this world—not just here in our tight-knit rural congregation but in the wider community in which we live, and in the city on which our livelihoods depend. It is true, we are not given a detailed description for how we should do this in each and every situation. How should we engage in the aftermath of all that has happened this week? I cannot say for certain. But if we are not given a description, we have been given a clear prescription. We must love one another. Surely God through the Holy Spirit will show us how.

And although it will not be easy—for love is never easy—we know now that it is not impossible. Love is possible because God first loved us. Love is possible because his mercy has dissolved our fears and hatreds. Love is possible because the resurrection assures us that Jesus has conquered sin. Love is possible because by his Spirit we continue to abide in the love of Christ. Indeed, he is never closer than when we love one another, just as he first loved us.

Rev. Andy Gathman serves as Pastor of Chestnut Grove Presbyterian Church, a congregation of 147 in Phoenix, MD, a few miles north of Baltimore in Baltimore County.

Love in the Season of Riots: Baltimore 2015

Christa Fuller Burns

> 1 John 4:7-21

What do you say on this particular Sunday? It seems over-whelming to respond to what we have experienced this week. So much has happened, and words seem feeble. We've felt despair, uncertainty, disgust, fear, disappointment, exhaustion, glimmers of hope, and moments of profound solidarity ... to name just a few of this week's mood swings. We've seen the best of who we are, and we've seen the worst. What do you say on this particular Sunday?

"In these turbulent days of uncertainty the evils of war and of economic and racial injustice threaten the very survival of the human race. Indeed, we live in a day of grave crisis."[2] These are the words that Martin Luther King wrote in the preface of a collection of his sermons, three of which he wrote in a Georgia jail. The name of the collection is *Strength to Love*, and it is striking to me that love is the predominant theme of a book written in what King calls "turbulent days of uncertainty."

I came back to this little book *Strength to Love* this week because, on the one hand, we have been reminded of the riots in 1968 in the aftermath of King's death, and we haven't been able to avoid the question of just how far we

---

[2] Martin Luther King, Jr. *Strength to Love* (Minneapolis: Augsburg Fortress, 1981).

have not come since then. On the other hand, I keep hearing Tina Turner belting out "What's Love Got to Do with It?"

When Deb and I drove down North Avenue on Friday on our way to the peace vigil and saw for ourselves what looked like a war zone, I wondered: what does love have to do with it? When we saw the fires and the looting, we wondered what's love got to do with it? When we heard what happened to Freddie Gray in that police van, we could ask what does love has to do with it? When we saw the volunteers out en masse cleaning up our neighborhoods, we could ask what's love got to do with it? When we saw a small boy handing out water to police with riot gear, we could ask what's love got to do with it?

What **does** love got to do with it?

According to the First Letter of John, love has quite a lot to do with it. In fact, maybe love has everything to do with it. Dear friends, let's love each other, because love is from God. Dear friends, if God loved us this way, we also ought to love each other. The author uses "Dear Friends" so much that we might be suspicious. Maybe those the letter was intended for were not such good friends. Maybe the author protests too much. We know that 1 John was written to folk who were not so sure about this whole love thing. Indeed, the temptation when reading this letter is to sentimentalize it, adorning it with hearts and flowers, concluding we just all need to get along, we just all need to love each other. It is that simple.

Let's go back to Dr. King, who said:

> When I speak of love I am not speaking of some sentimental and weak response. I am speaking of that force which all of the great

religions have seen as the supreme unifying principle of life. Love is somehow the key that unlocks the door which leads to ultimate reality. This Hindu-Muslim-Christian-Jewish-Buddhist belief about the ultimate reality is beautifully summed up in the first epistle of Saint John: "Let us love one another; for love is God and everyone that loveth is born of God and knoweth God."[3]

The word used in 1 John for love is "agape," that is love for the unworthy, the stranger, even love for the sinners. Agape is love for the community. In answer then to what's love got to do with it, according to John, love means love for rioters and looters. It means love for abusive police officers. It means love for small time drug dealers. It means love for the unloved all around us in Baltimore. Agape is not, in King's words, some sentimental and weak response.

I think it bears pointing out that 1 John was written to argue against a movement at the time which insisted that the way to salvation was to have some secret knowledge. Gnosticism argued that the way you knew if you loved God was if you knew the right creed, the right doctrines. We still have a lot of that kind of thinking around, don't we? You will be saved if you know what the Bible says about sin, about sexuality, about Jesus Christ's atoning death for our sins. We might say that it takes a secret knowledge to get a job in our city, or to get an education, or to avoid violent crime, or to get assistance when you are down on your luck.

---

[3] Martin Luther King Jr. "Why I Am Opposed to the War in Vietnam" (1967), p. 5.

There are those in the know; those who have secret knowledge ... and those who lack information.

John, on the other hand, says, no. It is not a matter of knowing the right stuff. It is not a matter of having some secret truth. Salvation is not based on knowledge at all ... but on love: "Everyone who loves ... knows God." I wish our Supreme Court could believe these words. I wish the jury deliberating in the Boston bombing case could hear these words. I wish people on the streets of Baltimore could hear these words. This is how we know God ... by our love.

Of course, one of the hardest obstacles to loving others, those so difficult to love, is fear. Fear was a strong emotion this week, wasn't it? On Monday, I stayed at the office late because that is what I do on book group nights. I stay in the office until 7:00 p.m. because I find that I can get a lot done in those two hours. However, on Monday, people were texting and calling about what was going on downtown, and all of a sudden it occurred to me that I was the only person in the building. My car was the only car in the parking lot. I had this palpable sense of fear. And, I have to admit, to a slight twinge of trepidation when we drove along North Avenue on Friday and people were spilling out into the streets and we passed armored tanks, national guards people, and burned out buildings ... and the chanting pulsed all around us.

We have to admit this morning that we've been afraid ... afraid for our city, for uncontrolled violence, for destruction, for the realization that something is really badly broken, and we don't know how to fix it. We've been afraid.

Perhaps, then, what John has to say to us this morning, of all mornings is: "There is no fear in love, but perfect love drives out fear."

At our prayer vigil on Friday, the Rev. Tanya Wade led us in a prayer for peace, using the story of Jesus and his friends out on the sea when the storm came. You remember that story? Jesus and the disciples go out on a boat at dusk and, as is not unusual for the Sea of Galilee, a sudden storm comes up. The boat is swamped by the raging sea. Meanwhile, Jesus is sound asleep on a pillow. Don't you care, Jesus? Don't you care that we are all about to die, demand the disciples? How could you just sleep through this? Jesus wakes up and tells the sea "Peace! Be still!" The wind stops, the waves become placid again. Jesus wants to know, "Why are you so afraid? Have you still no faith?" (Mark 4:35-40)

Indeed, when the storms come and the times are turbulent and there is uncertainty and, in King's words, "economic and racial injustice threaten" our very survival, as they surely do now, why are we so afraid? Don't we have faith?

I guess we are not perfect yet. God is still working on us. The Good News is that love can be perfected in us. Love can be perfected in us.

So, this is our job now. Let us work on getting that perfect love that casts out fear. Let us work on loving our brothers and sisters completely, without fear. Indeed, let us work on loving our enemies. We can do this. Yes, we can. Because God first loved us!

The Rev. Christa Fuller Burns serves as Pastor at Faith Presbyterian Church, a 152-member congregation in northeastern Baltimore City, which also houses the offices of Baltimore Presbytery.

The Fields of Mondamin

Kenneth E. Kovacs

> 'I am the true vine, and my Father is the vine-grower. He removes every branch in me that bears no fruit. Every branch that bears fruit he prunes to make it bear more fruit. You have already been cleansed by the word that I have spoken to you. Abide in me as I abide in you. Just as the branch cannot bear fruit by itself unless it abides in the vine, neither can you unless you abide in me. I am the vine, you are the branches. Those who abide in me and I in them bear much fruit, because apart from me you can do nothing. Whoever does not abide in me is thrown away like a branch and withers; such branches are gathered, thrown into the fire, and burned. If you abide in me, and my words abide in you, ask for whatever you wish, and it will be done for you. My Father is glorified by this, that you bear much fruit and become my disciples. John 15:1-11

The story goes that one day the great American poet Henry Wadsworth Longfellow (1807-1855) arrived in Baltimore to visit his friend Dr. Patrick Macaulay (1795-1849), physician, city councilman, B & O Railroad director, patron of the arts. He lived on a seventy-three-acre plantation, purchased in 1827, situated on the hills above Baltimore harbor. Dr. Macaulay had yet to come up with a name for his "estate" and so he asked Longfellow to suggest one. Looking around and seeing field upon field of corn growing everywhere, Longfellow replied, "Why not Mondamin, after the Indian corn god?" Mapmakers eventually added a "w" to the name. That's how we know it today. After the events of this week in Baltimore, that's how people all around the nation, indeed the world know it today. Perhaps you've never heard of Mondawmin or never driven past the shopping mall named for the neighborhood or never shopped there (I know it well and shop there often), but we all know where it is now.

Nothing is left of the plantation house, which was known as "the pink house." As a footnote, Mondawnin was sold, after Macaulay's death, in 1850, to George Brown (1787-1859), chairman of Alex Brown and Sons, the first investment bank in the United States, who preserved the plantation. He was a Presbyterian. Brown Memorial Presbyterian Church in Bolton Hill was dedicated in memory of him in 1870. The last private owner of the Mondawmin estate was Alexander Brown, who died there in 1949.

Baltimore's first urban mall opened in Mondawmin in 1956. Its coffee shop, called The White Coffee Pot, did not serve blacks.[4] By 1957 the area was already changing and after the 1968 riots the neighborhood, along with the mall, seriously declined.

The Mondawmin neighborhood is bounded by Longwood Street and Hilton Parkway to the west, Liberty Heights Avenue and Druid Park Drive to the north, Druid Hill Park and Fulton Avenue to the east, and North Avenue to the south. These have become familiar street names to the wider world: Fulton Street, North Avenue. North

---

[4] Antero Pietila, *Not in My Neighborhood: How Bigotry Shaped a Great American City* (Chicago: Ivan R. Dee, 2010), 122.

Avenue and Pennsylvania, the epicenter of this week's protests and police presence, is just on the edge of the Mondawmin neighborhood as it flows into the Sandtown-Winchester neighborhood to the south. Drive south on Fulton Street and it eventually crosses Presstman Street, the location of the Gilmor Homes, where Freddie Gray was arrested.

Longfellow tells us in The Song of Hiawatha that the god Manito was intent on helping Hiawatha care for the needs of his people. And so Manito sent help. "Who are you?" Hiawatha whispered. "I am Mondamin," the young man answered. "Manito has sent me to answer your prayers. He wants you to know your people will always have food. But they must work hard for it. And now you must work. You must wrestle with me." After wrestling with him seven times Mondamin fell and was buried in the ground. He became one with the ground and from his ashes new growth, corn stalks rose from the ground to feed the people. Hence, Mondamin became known as the corn god.

It's there, in the former fields of Mondawmin, that we see the yield of seeds sown by of our racist, segregationist past. Today, growing in the fields or living in the streets and alleys of Mondawmin, the City of Baltimore is reaping what it has sown for decades, generations. It's complex, extremely complex.

There isn't one core problem, but many, a rat's nest of problems that seem to coalesce around one central issue: *economic disparity*. The deep sin of racism cannot be overlooked. Antero Pietela's book, *Not in My Neighborhood: How Bigotry shaped a Great American City*, tells the sordid story of Baltimore's segregationist and anti-Semitic history (which are linked). Racism permeates everything, but it doesn't explain everything that we have witnessed this week. While we must in no way condone the violence of this week, it is our responsibility as Christians, as people called to weep with those who weep and rejoice with those who rejoice (Romans 12:15), to act with empathy and compassion as we try to place ourselves in the life of someone who lives in Sandtown in order to understand the rage.

If you've never driven through that part of the city, I encourage you to do so—not at this moment, of course, but soon. There's block after block of urban blight. There are "16,000 vacant houses" in Baltimore and "roughly 14,000 empty lots" in the city. "The area that saw the worst rioting this week is far more intact than some neighborhoods, where whole blocks of row houses are dead but not gone."[5] The families that live there are "*trapped*...some of the poorest in the country, where low tax revenue means less money for schools, which means poor education, which leads to few or no good jobs, which leads to alternative and often illegal ways to put food on the table, which leads to prison, which leads to broken homes, which begins the cycle of desperation all over again." This is how James B. Parks, vice-moderator of Baltimore Presbytery, very helpfully summarized the situation at the prayer vigil on Friday.

Close to 100 Presbyterians gathered on Friday afternoon, outdoors on an empty lot beside Trinity Presbyterian Church, an African-American church near Walbrook Junction, about a mile west of Mondawmin Mall. It was a diverse crowd. We gathered to sing, pray, light candles for justice and peace. And we prayed for *everyone*. Petition after petition was lifted up for everyone: from the innocent children to parents to school teachers to store owners; and we prayed for those now out of work because

---

[5] Eugene Robinson, in *Washington Post*, April 30, 2015.

of the destruction, the poor living conditions in the city, the inequality, the urban blight, the police officers and national guard members, firemen, care providers, the city council, the mayor, the state's attorney, the governor, victims of violence and brutality, people on the edge of it all who don't understand or won't try to understand. We prayed for justice, peace, healing, reconciliation, and forgiveness. The presbytery promised that the service on Friday would not be an isolated event. There are churches in the city that have heard all of these prayers and expressions of concern from predominantly white Presbyterians before, for decades. We vowed that this would not be a one-off event, but the start of something new, different.

It was a marvelous expression of the church of Jesus Christ being the church. We were sowing seeds of hope, I believe, hope for something new to yield in the fields of Mondawmin. Jesus said people will be able to identify his followers by the fruit that they bear, by the yield. We're supposed to bear fruit, yield something with our lives. "I am the vine, you are the branches. Those who abide in me and I in them bear much fruit, for apart from me you can do nothing" (John 15:5). And God is glorified when we, as God's children, bear fruit—not *some* fruit, "*much* fruit." And the essential fruit that we are called to yield is love (John 15:9). That is the sign that we abide in Jesus and that he abides in us.

And sometimes for love to be enacted, for a branch to yield new growth it needs to be pruned. I'm not sure if the actual act of pruning hurts the vine. Can the vine "feel" it? I don't know. It certainly sounds painful. But, as we all know, there's no growth without pruning. I would like to think that the events of this week will become a kind of pruning for all of us, white and black, rich and poor, city and county dweller, most notably the church of Jesus Christ, both the so-called "liberal" and "conservative" church, alike. It's been said that one of the roles of the church, one of the tasks of preaching is to "comfort the afflicted and afflict the comforted." We're not called to afflict the comforted just to be mean to them or to judge. It's offered in love. It's a kind of pruning, which wakes people up, quickens one's conscience, opens up one's heart and mind, which then gives us the capacity to listen—really listen—for what the Spirit is calling us to be and do, calling us to really *love*. We all need pruning at times.

As we approach the Lord's Table this morning, with the images of this past week still fresh and raw, and in light of those events, here are two questions to consider: what fruit will you bear in your personal lives? And as for the church, what will be our yield?

> **Rev. Kenneth E. Kovacs** is Pastor at Catonsville Presbyterian Church, a congregation of 415 members in the southwestern suburbs of Baltimore.

Just Sad

Alison Halsey

John 15:1-8

As of an hour ago I decided not to preach the sermon I had originally planned to preach this Sunday. It is sitting on my desk. I am incredibly sad this week, and I need to speak from my heart.

As most of you know I was pastor of First & Franklin Presbyterian Church in downtown Baltimore for thirteen years before coming here as your interim pastor. I have spent most of my ministry being an urban pastor, and so watching and hearing of the riots on Monday evening broke my heart. I recognized where they were filming; I knew people who lived in some of the neighborhoods. I found myself watching the TV through tear-filled eyes and praying. I so much wanted to get in my car and return to my previous congregation, but I am no longer its pastor.

But this morning I would like to share with you some observations from that church's ministry and mission. It may shed some light on why I believe we witnessed what we did on Monday evening. The frustration is far deeper than the death of Freddie Grey.

The church had a relationship with the Samuel Coleridge Taylor Elementary School on the western side of Martin Luther King Blvd. At one point we rebuilt their library, we collected books for the school, tried to support the teachers, helped create a butterfly garden for them, and bought uniforms and school supplies for the children who could not afford them. It was a wonderful school, with dedicated teachers and a creative hardworking principal. At more than one of our meetings he said his goal was to save these children. He believed the parents of his students were lost to the world of drugs, and their chances of knowing another life were slim to none. So he worked with the grandparents and aunts and others who were responsible for his students in an effort to give them hope and support. I could only imagine what these awesome children had seen and experienced.

Another situation involving children: The church sat between two shelters—one for adolescent girls placed there primarily by the juvenile justice system (it was run by an organization and supported by a foundation of the church), and a home for boys ages 8 through 14 run by another organization. Each summer we ran a week or two-week summer arts program for the boys. We served them dinner, sang songs with them, allowed them to be children and taught them a new art skill from sewing to puppets to mosaics to painting. It was great fun and the counselors were amazed at how attentive the boys were. Every year we also sponsored their Christmas party at the church. We also hosted programs for the girls. These homes were good! Children were given a safe and secure place to be; they were taught new ways of seeing themselves, educated in life skills, challenged to academically succeed, and most importantly, given hope and love. Unfortunately, the state in an effort to save money decided not to fund this way of helping this population of children. They came up with a money-saving brilliant (?) plan. Under the guise of restoring the family unit, they planned to return these children to their very dysfunctional homes and provide what they called 'wrap around care.' This meant social workers and educators would be sent in to work with the families as a whole.

Sounds like a good plan? With the exception that these children were removed from their homes for pretty dire reasons, and I didn't see the state funding additional social workers to make this happen. We saved money at what expense, and very few spoke up for the children. I wondered how many of those fantastic boys were involved in the rioting.

We also worked with the Sandtown Habitat for Humanity rebuilding houses. I know what these neighborhoods look like, with boarded up buildings, few playgrounds and stores, and littered empty lots. A far cry from where we sit this morning.

One last story. The church was also involved with a shelter for men who were recently released from jail and were recovering from drug or alcohol addictions. The shelter was in a church-owned home on our campus and was heavily supported by it. Every year we hosted their holiday party in one of our other buildings. At the end of this event I was getting ready to leave and needed someone to walk me to the church's parking lot (around the corner and down a dark alley road—not a real safe place for a lone woman to walk). I asked and two of the men from the home immediately sprung up and said they would be glad to accompany me. As we rounded the corner and headed up the alley (a large African American man on each side of me) I joked with them about never having felt quite so safe. One of the men said to me, "I don't feel safe at all. You do know that if a police car came around the corner and saw this scene—two large black men on either side of this older, small white woman—they would shoot first and ask questions later." Wow, he was so right.

And so I am sad this morning because we have created these riots in so many, many ways, and most of us are just so unaware of all the issues involved. I do know that Jesus is sad as well and that his spirit walked with the clergy who braved the crowd and police to bring order to the riots.

In the scripture lesson for today, Jesus said, "I am the true vine, and my father is the vine grower. He removes every branch in me that bears no fruit. Every branch that bears fruit he prunes to make it bear more fruit."

Vineyards take a major amount of work and pruning. Three or four times a year people are sent into vineyards to prune. It is done by hand, and it is time consuming. All this pruning Jesus speaks of is for two purposes—one, that we abide in him who is considered to be the trunk or the core of the vine and two, that we bear fruit. Changing the environment in our cities, in our neighborhoods will be difficult. Racism is deep seated. There is much work to be done to right the past and come to the place where all God's children are treated equally and with respect.

If we are serious at all about abiding in Christ, then we had better be prepared for some serious pruning of our lives, which will center us back to the love of God. It is difficult, I will be the first to admit, to prune off those areas of our lives which are draining the vitality out of us in nonproductive ways rather than allowing us to be fruitful. And we had better be prepared to commit ourselves to growing in new ways because this vine may branch off in new directions making us uncomfortable. It might involve us in seriously looking at the issues facing our state and our communities and how in many ways we may be contributing to the problems.

What about us? What might we do? There are similar situations not so far away in Annapolis. Might we trim back a bit and instead work with others and join some tutoring programs for children in the Annapolis schools or ask some of our sister African American Presbyterian churches in Baltimore how we might be able to help them? Or spend a little time speaking with some leaders in our community about the problems which are first and foremost and seek some ways to solve these. Start small—branches which are strong and produce fruit began as tiny buds and then grew. If we are attached to the vine, we will blossom and grow.

May you, may we as a congregation, do some pruning so we might be able to follow in the footsteps of Christ and be awakened to the Spirit of God. May this difficult time help us to discover what needs to be released so the new life of Christ springing up within us might bear fruit to ease this pain and sorrow.

May the peace of Christ disturb us into action.

The Rev. Alison Halsey is a Teaching Elder in Baltimore Presbytery, having served as Pastor of First & Franklin Street Presbyterian Church, and most recently, as Interim Pastor of Christ Our Anchor Presbyterian Church in Annapolis, where this sermon was preached.

Life Together: Branches of the Vine

John V. Carlson

John 15:1-8

So, unlike the way it always is in the fictional village Lake Wobegon that we hear about on *A Prairie Home Companion*, it has *not* been a quiet week here. For me personally, it would have been a very busy week even under ideal circumstances: there was a Vacation Bible School meeting on Monday night to plan our summer program; I had a meeting Tuesday afternoon of the Emergency Food and Shelter Funding program; on Wednesday there was a Mission and Stewardship Team meeting to address some of our financial concerns, followed immediately by Praise Team and Choir; Saturday morning early I chaired our monthly Harford Hammers board meeting, and then spent the rest of the day with teams from Highland and other Presbyterian churches in our area in a workshop on better communications in the parish. In between times, I was writing newsletter articles, planning for our Porcupine benefit concert on May 17, and oh yes, trying to write this sermon.

A busy week under ideal circumstances—and then came the events in Baltimore: disturbing, sad, painful to watch and to think about. And when upsetting events happen many states away, we can sometimes turn away and say, "Well, I'm glad it's not here. That's not our problem." But when it happens here in our own back yard, we realize it is our problem.

And so that became part of my week, too: helping to plan and lead a prayer service on Tuesday night, attending a prayer vigil in Baltimore on Friday. But it's not just the toll taken by the time and effort involved in planning and attending events; even more, it's the way the violence and sadness and general uneasiness get inside you, and stay with you, and dominate your thinking. It makes you examine your faith and search for answers.

And I found it also affected my thinking about all the other normal church tasks and duties in two interesting ways, for on the one hand, it puts everything else in perspective: the endless round of meetings and administrative tasks and even sermons seem small by comparison to the burdens borne by police and firefighters and community leaders and elected officials and everyday men and women trying to get their neighborhoods and their city back under control. But on the other hand, it makes those same meetings and tasks and duties seem all the more important, for these are the things which help to give our fellowship and our own community meaning and order. And I know I could find agreement here, because at all those meetings I talked about, including the Tuesday night prayer service, members of this church were present, participating, planning, praying, that Christian life together in this community will be what God intended for it to be, in sending Jesus Christ to call us here together.

Such a grand goal is surely too much for any of us to bear alone, and indeed, we may sometimes feel very discouraged. By now you all know that we are currently facing some fairly serious financial challenges; I'm personally hopeful here, but we all have to step up to make things work. But the challenge is not just financial: several people observed to me independently just this past week that people seem tired, burned out even.

It got me to wondering if that's what Jesus observe at that last sad supper with his disciples. As he looks around the table into the faces of his followers, he sees the sadness in their eyes, hears the anxiety in their questions, knows that they have not yet fully understood their roles. He knows that they have not yet fully understood what their relationship with him is to be like, especially when he is gone. And so he tells them, *I am the vine, you are the branches. Those who abide in me and I in them bear much fruit, because apart from me you can do nothing. ... But ... if you abide in me, and my words abide in you, ask for whatever you wish, and it will be done for you.*

These words certainly speak to me—and I hope to you—as we think about the goals and tasks that are before us: dealing with meetings, with money, with membership losses—all require commitment from us and a willingness to work hard and to sacrifice. But we cannot hope to be the believers Christ calls us to be apart from a relationship with him: one that each of us cultivates on our own, as one leaf, or as one branch of a vine. But even more importantly, we cannot begin to imagine life together as a community, as a church family, apart from that organic relationship with one another in our faith in Jesus Christ. We are branches on the vine, connected to one another through him.

But this is not just about how to attend to the institutional aspects of being a church—managing finances, holding worship, dealing with the needs of our membership. This is about how to be the church in the world. This is about how the church carries out its mission in the world: this is how clergy and church leaders could be on the front lines in Baltimore this past week; this is how pastors were able to work side by side with gang members to make sure kids got on the buses safely Thursday morning when schools reopened. Christians were able to be there in those tense and even dangerous situations because they know they are not acting alone; they are branches on a vine. This is how we do mission trips and run a clothing closet and even play bingo with Alzheimer's patients. Branches on the vine.

And this is how we live the Christian life as we go our ways after we leave this place: for we must remain branches on the vine even when we are not within these walls: This is what enables us to speak up when we see something wrong; this is what empowers us to stand against the prevailing trends in our society like racism, or materialism, or hatred or fear. We are branches on the vine, as Jesus tells us, *I am the vine, you are the branches. Those who abide in me and I in them bear much fruit, because apart from me you can do nothing.* And by the same token, *If you abide in me, and my words abide in you, ask for whatever you wish, and it will be done for you.*

As we come to the table this morning, let it be the first step for each of us to being grafted anew on to that one, true vine; may the true vine-grower be the One to prune away the sin and to nourish our spirits, that we may bear much fruit. Amen.

The Rev. John V. Carlson currently serves as Vice-Moderator of the Presbytery of Baltimore; he is retired after serving for 13 years as Pastor at Highland Presbyterian Church, a rural congregation of 200 in northern Harford County, about 40 miles from Baltimore, where this communion meditation was delivered.

Things That Defile

Stephen R. Melton

Then he called the crowd to him and said to them, "Listen and understand: it is not what goes into the mouth that defiles a person, but it is what comes out of the mouth that defiles." Then the disciples approached and said to him, "Do you know that the Pharisees took offense when they heard what you said?" He answered, "Every plant that my heavenly Father has not planted will be uprooted. Let them alone; they are blind guides of the blind. And if one blind person guides another, both will fall into a pit." But Peter said to him, "Explain this parable to us." Then he said, "Are you also still without understanding? Do you not see that whatever goes into the mouth enters the stomach, and goes out into the sewer? But what comes out of the mouth proceeds from the heart, and this is what defiles. For out of the heart come evil intentions, murder, adultery, fornication, theft, false witness, slander. These are what defile a person, but to eat with unwashed hands does not defile." Matthew 15: 10 – 20

Coming from New York State, I have noticed the weather patterns here are somewhat different. When I lived in Pennsylvania, we would pay attention to the weather reports out west in Indiana. We knew that whatever was happening there was going to make its way to us in the east in about two days, but you couldn't predict the weather in

New York, and, it seems, it can be pretty difficult to predict the weather here in Maryland as well.

There is also another kind of weather we cannot entirely predict: the weather of our culture. Without much notice, the barometric pressure for kindness can drop and the clouds of sarcasm can settle in. One day it can be relatively calm and peaceful, and then the next day a young man is arrested in the streets of Baltimore, and before long it is like a hurricane blew through our city.

And, like a hurricane, there can be damage to families and to homes and to properties, but there seems to be another kind of damage which is hard to put our finger on, but just as hurtful as when Jesus told Thomas to stick a finger in his side.

The storm in our community landed with the death of Freddie Gray. Really doesn't matter for whom we feel a particular kinship—we have all felt some of the negative after-effects.

The image which comes to mind is of a creek bed—the kind where we can look down and the water seems clear enough—then when we step into it, all of sudden the bottom gets stirred up. It goes from being crystal clear to being a muddy mess in a matter of seconds.

I feel like that is what happened to us. Our pond had been relatively clear, but with the death of Freddie Grey, now there is a murky awfulness. Maybe all these negative feelings were already there—like mud on the floor of the creek bed, but now angers and hurts and frustrations, and Lord only know what else, are circulating around us.

Suddenly, we are in a muddy mess.

In some ways, there is nothing much we can do about this present muck—the cultural water is muddy, and it will take some time for a divine current to make things better. For a time, this is how it will be.

And yet, there are some things we can do.

One thing we can do is be careful not to pollute the waters any further. It is so easy to muddy the waters with ungenerous comments.

It is so harsh out there, so muddy, if we happen to say something negative, our comment just becomes more of the muck.

But maybe we can do a little something to help clear the water. I think of the Frederick Douglas High School students who marched with signs saying they loved their city, or the members of the Baltimore orchestra who stepped outside the safe walls of the Meyerhoff amphitheater to play for free just to show their love for their community.

Maybe there are things we can do.

In the scripture today the Pharisees are preoccupied with the muddiness of the waters around Jesus and his disciples. In their messy world, they want Jesus and the disciples to be more attentive to the purity laws.

Yet Jesus doesn't cotton to their concerns much. In fact, he fusses at them for spending so much time with trying to avoid the messiness of it all.

For Jesus, the real dirt is not what we get on our hands; the real dirt is what comes out of our mouths.

In the end, Jesus wasn't as concerned with cultural purity because he wants us out in the world so God can use the very culture we fear to change US.

We may not be able to alter our culture any more than we can alter the path of a tornado, but we can alter how we respond to them.

At one time we thought the best Christians were those who separated themselves from the world. But the wisest monks will tell you the greatest evil they have to contend with is not in their culture but in their own hearts. There is where the battle is fought.

That is what Jesus is after.

In the Preparation [see below] today I use something from the Jewish Midrash on the levels of charity. You see, on the one hand, it really doesn't matter why we do something kind. We might be doing it for all the "wrong" reasons. Maybe we want to make ourselves feel proud or better than others. But, even if we have the wrong motivations, in some ways, it doesn't matter as long as the hungry person is fed, the cold person is warmed, the lonely person is visited.

At the first levels of charity the person does something good, but it is less good because it shows disrespect. It is still good, though, because someone is now less hungry and now someone is less cold. It is the **lowest** level of goodness, but it is better than **no** goodness.

Think about this: Have you ever known someone who said they didn't want to do a something good because they were not sure their motivation was good—and so they end up doing nothing at all?!

We can't let ourselves get too caught up in acting from a pure motivation. We need to do good even if for the wrong reasons. God knows we have mixed motivations, and yet God still needs us to help heal the world—even if we have dirty hands. It is better to do something good for the wrong reason than to do nothing at all.

But here is where Jesus speaks a deeper word.

Even though on the one hand, the motivations of our heart don't matter—for ***their*** soul—on the other hand it makes all the difference for **our** soul.

As we read through the levels of charity, we can hear Jesus. Regardless of how pure we seem on the outside, he wants to purify our soul. Do the right thing for the right reason.

Jesus knows our motivations are not always perfect. We are often swirling around in dirty waters of our culture. We are not pure.

Yet, our purity is his business really, not ours. He is working on it.

Our business is to serve him.

His business is to change our hearts.

We set our hearts straight for God's will. God will set our hearts straight.

To God be the glory. Forever and ever. Amen.

The Rev. Stephen Melton pastors the Churchville Presbyterian Church, a 150-member church in rural Harford County, MD, approximately 25 miles northeast of the city of Baltimore.

The following material appeared in the church's worship bulletin the day this sermon was preached.

PREPARATION

In her book, *My Grandfather's Blessings*, Rachel Remen talks about the levels of charity. According to the Jewish Mishnah, which is a collection of wisdom teachings, there are eight levels of "charity"—another word for "love."

> I want to give you a examples of those eight levels.
>
> At the eighth, or the lowest level, a homeless man asks a man for a coat; the man begrudgingly buys a coat for the man who asks for help. He makes sure to do it in the presence of witnesses so others will see just how loving he is, and he waits to be thanked.
>
> At the seventh level, he does the same thing, except he doesn't wait to be asked.
>
> At the sixth level, he helps the man except he does it with an open heart and without hesitation.
>
> At the fifth level, he kindly gives the man the coat, but he does it in private where others cannot see.
>
> At the forth level, he warmly gives the man his own coat, not one he bought, and he does it in private.
>
> At the third level, the man gives away his coat, but this time to a man who does not know who gave him the coat.

At the second level, the man gives away his coat and does not know who receives it.

At the highest level of giving, a man gladly gives away his own coat without knowing who will receive it and the person who receives it doesn't know who gave it to him. His giving is the natural expression of goodness. He gives without thought or regret, as naturally as flowers breathe out perfume and their colors bring beauty to God's good earth.[6]

---

[6] Rachel Naomi Remen, *My Grandfather's Blessings* (Riverhead Books 2001) 86-87.

Why Are You Afraid?

Tanya Denley

Now the Philistines gathered their armies for battle. ... And there came out from the camp of the Philistines a champion named Goliath. ... He stood and shouted to the ranks of Israel ... 'Choose a man for yourselves, and let him come down to me. If he is able to fight with me and kill me, then we will be your servants; but if I prevail against him and kill him, then you shall be our servants and serve us.' ...

David rose early in the morning [and] came to the encampment as the army was going forth to the battle line. ... [Goliath] came up out of the ranks of the Philistines, and spoke the same words as before. ... David said to Saul, 'Let no one's heart fail because of him; your servant will go and fight with this Philistine.' Saul said to David, 'You are not able to go against this Philistine to fight with him; for you are just a boy, and he has been a warrior from his youth.' But David said to Saul, 'Your servant used to keep sheep for his father. ... Your servant has killed both lions and bears; and this uncircumcised Philistine shall be like one of them, since he has defied the armies of the living God. ... The Lord, who saved me from the paw of the lion and from the paw of the bear, will save me from the hand of this Philistine.' So Saul said to David, 'Go, and may the Lord be with you!'

Saul clothed David with his armor; he put a bronze helmet on his head and clothed him with a coat of mail. David strapped Saul's sword over the armor, and he tried in vain to walk, for he was not used to them. Then David said to Saul, 'I cannot walk with these; for I am not used to them.' So David removed them. Then he took his staff in his hand, and chose five smooth stones from the wadi, and put them in his shepherd's bag, in the pouch; his sling was in his hand, and he drew near to the Philistine.

The Philistine came on and drew near to David. ... When the Philistine looked and saw David, he disdained him, for he was only a youth. ... The Philistine said to David, 'Am I a dog, that you come to me with sticks?' And the Philistine cursed David by his gods. ... But David said to the Philistine, 'You come to me with sword and spear and javelin; but I come to you in the name of the Lord of hosts, the God of the armies of Israel, whom you have defied. This very day the Lord will deliver you into my hand, and I will strike you down and cut off your head; and I will give the dead bodies of the Philistine army this very day to the birds of the air and to the wild animals of the earth, so that all the earth may know that there is a God in Israel, and that all this assembly may know that the Lord does not save by sword and spear; for the battle is the Lord's and he will give you into our hand.'

When the Philistine drew nearer to meet David, David ran quickly towards the battle line to meet the Philistine. David put his hand in his bag, took out a stone, slung it, and struck the Philistine on his forehead; the stone sank into his forehead, and he fell face down on the ground. 1 Samuel 17: 1-49 Selected Verses

On that day, when evening had come, he said to them, 'Let us go across to the other side.' And leaving the crowd behind, they took him with them in the boat, just as he was. Other boats were with him. A great gale arose, and the waves beat into the boat, so that the boat was already being swamped. But he was in the stern, asleep on the cushion; and they woke him up and said to him, 'Teacher, do you not care that we are perishing?' He woke up and rebuked the wind, and said to the sea, 'Peace! Be still!' Then the wind ceased, and there was a dead calm. He said to them, 'Why are you afraid? Have you still no faith?' And they were filled with great awe and said to one another, 'Who then is this, that even the wind and the sea obey him?' Mark 4:35-41

I opened my Facebook feed on Friday morning and one of the first things I saw was a clip from Jon Stewart's Daily Show on Thursday night. If you haven't seen it, I recommend it.

Stewart says, "I have one job, and it's a pretty simple job. I come in, in the morning, and we look at the news, and I write jokes about it.

"But I didn't do my job today, so I apologize. I got nothing for you in terms of jokes and sounds, because of what happened in South Carolina. And so, I honestly have nothing other than just sadness once again that we have to peer into the abyss of the depraved violence that we do to each other and the nexus of a just gaping racial wound that will not heal yet we pretend doesn't exist."

And so I have one job this morning, to preach the Good News of Jesus Christ. And I stand before you today, a 40-year-old white woman who was born in the South, grew up in Memphis, TN and Birmingham, AL who learned about the "War of Northern Aggression" in my high school history class. I stand before you, a church that has been active in the civil rights movement, with parishioners who sat down in Greensboro, with parishioners who put their life on the line for civil rights, and with parishioners who are still putting their lives on the line, and being active in the movement today. I stand before you aware of Jon Stewart's words-

"And I'm confident, though, that by acknowledging it, by staring into that [just gaping racial wound] and seeing it for what it is, we still won't do jack s—. Yeah. That's us ..."

And all I can do today, is to stare into that wound and start to do something about it.

I truly believe that God works in mysterious ways. And those mysterious ways led to me standing before you today. For the preacher who agreed to be here today had a last minute conflict, and Rev. Kanahan then picked my name off of the supply preacher list, and asked me to preach—without knowing anything about me. And here I stand before you with the lectionary this morning being David and Goliath and the story of Jesus stilling the sea.

I want to start with the story of David and Goliath—and I want us to think about the story anew—try to imagine being one of the Israelites there in that valley.

Imagine waiting for the battle, and a Philistine, a giant, named Goliath comes up and challenges you and your fellow soldiers to fight—a fight to the death, which might avert a major battle, one life for the sake of many. And you look at this giant, who towers over you and the other Israelites, who has the best swords and shields that money has to offer. And he is looking for a challenger and offers—"If he is able to fight with me and kill me, then we will be your servants; but if I prevail against him and kill him, then you shall be our servants and serve us."

Would you be willing to go forth? Would you look to your fellow soldier to go forth, or would you take a step back?

And then, this ruddy youth, just a boy really, offers to fight for the Israelites—you look at him as he steps forward towards Goliath- and see that he's not wearing any armor at all. You see him pick up five rocks from the wadi, put them in his bag and walk towards Goliath.

And you hear in the background the servants repeating the conversation between David and Saul—your king—when David offered to fight this giant. And how David is just a shepherd—a shepherd tending to the flock—and you hear the servants laugh for David said: "Your servant has killed both lions and bears; and this uncircumcised Philistine shall be like one of them, since he has defied the armies of the living God." They can't imagine this young boy, this shepherd killing lions and bears.

But then the servants get serious again and quote David who said, "The LORD, who saved me from the paw of the lion and from the paw of the bear, will save me from the hand of this Philistine."

The servants say there was something in his voice, something that made you want to believe, something that made them trust that this young shepherd could possibly go and fight this giant. So Saul sent David on his way "Go, and may the LORD be with you!" And so you edge closer to see this shepherd go against the giant. Maybe, just maybe this shepherd can fight the giant.

And then you hear the giant speak—in his deep voice, making fun of David and cursing David by his gods—yet in a clear voice—deeper than you expected, and more melodic. David responds:

> *You come to me with sword and spear and javelin; but I come to you in the name of the LORD of hosts, the God of the armies of Israel, whom you have defied. This very day the LORD will deliver you into my hand, and I will strike you down ... so that all the earth may know that there is a God in Israel, and that all this assembly may know that the LORD does not save by sword and spear; for the battle is the Lord's and he will give you into our hand.*

And you believe David for you hear something in his voice, something that made you trust him that the Lord was with him and that the Lord would protect him.

And I wonder if that is the same voice the disciples knew and expected from Jesus. For the disciples were afraid, in the boat, with the waves crashing into the boat. And Jesus slept on, undisturbed.

The disciple woke him, crying, Teacher do you not care that we are perishing?

Teacher, do you not care that we are perishing? Teacher, do you not see the nine bodies lying in the church, the man lying in the middle of the street, the many being taken out of the police van who can't breathe, the child lying on the ground in a hoodie, and even the four little girls buried in rubble? God, do you not see the white people asleep, undisturbed by the storm that is raging around them? Do you not see that they sleep while we are dying?

God, why do you say, Why are you afraid? Do you still have no faith? How can we have faith when your house, the house of the Lord, is not safe, when we are not safe in our own neighborhood or our own homes? How can we still have faith, when we are fighting for our lives each and every day, and the world sleeps on undisturbed?

Now I can't speak for God, and I can't truly answer these questions, but maybe the story of David and Goliath can help us find the answer.

Goliath was looking for a challenger, someone to fight—someone who was his equal. And David stepped forth to fight. And it seems David was the exact opposite of what Goliath was looking for. David was a shepherd, a simple herder, one who did not fight, one whose life was not on the battle field.

Yet David perhaps was the best prepared, for he fought not to fight or even to win. He fought for God, to show all the earth that there is a God in Israel and a God who protects his people. David fought for God and he fought how he knew how, not in the ways of soldiers, but in the ways of shepherds, with simple rocks.

And maybe this is a guide for us—maybe we are called not to fight in the ways we see around us—with violence and hate, with fear and distrust. Maybe we are called to fight with love and faith, truth and trust. Maybe we are called to be like disciples waking those around us who slumber and maybe we are called to speak the truth in love—to show that God created us all in God's image—that we are all beloved children of God.

I wish I could say today that this will close that gaping racial wound, but I'm afraid it won't. But maybe by building relationships with those within your church community and then outside the church walls with those in your surrounding community—learning what their concerns are, what their gifts and dreams are and sharing your concerns, gifts and dreams are for your community—we can start the healing process.

And maybe just as David was called to use his voice and his words to fight the giant, we too are called to speak God's words and God's truth. We need to speak out and name things as they are—to call this shooting in Charleston an act of terror, and the product of generations of hatred and fear of the other. We need to name the places in our lives and our society where we see fear, where we see privilege, where we see hate. And that also means we need to look at ourselves and root out those places in ourselves where we see privilege, where we see fear and where we see hate.

And if we do these things, we will begin to heal—we will begin to see God's kingdom on earth. We will, like David, overcome the giant, and like the disciples, survive the storm.

So will you stand with me today, staring into that just gaping racial wound and seeing it for what it is, seeing where God's body is broken in the world today, and start to speak God's words and God's truth to bring forth God's kingdom on earth?

The Rev. Tanya J. Denley is a Teaching Elder in Baltimore Presbytery and has most recently served as Chaplain at Mercy Hospital and as Parish Associate at Dickey Memorial Presbyterian Church, both in Baltimore.

Five Smooth Stones

Jeanne E. Gay

1 Samuel 17:38-40 and Mark 4:35-41

We begin with lamentation. Is there one among us whose heart didn't break this week when we learned of the young shooter who killed nine people gathered for Bible study? Bible Study! Shouldn't we be safe when we gather to study God's word?

Lamentation. The words of the prophet Jeremiah ring true for us.

> *O that my head were a spring of water,*
> *and my eyes a fountain of tears,*
> *so that I might weep day and night*
> *for the slain of my poor people!* (Jer 9:1)

But there's more going on for us than lamentation. This was not a tsunami or a hurricane—a natural event, an "act of God." No, this time it was a young man choosing to go into a church with a long history of seeking justice for black people in this country. A church where he chose to sit with the people in prayer and in the study God's Word—the parable of the sower, I understand—and then he chose to shoot and kill nine of them.

> Cynthia Hurd
>
> Susie Jackson
>
> Ethel Lance
>
> DePayn Middleton-Doctor
>
> The Honorable Rev. Clementa Pinckney

Tywanza Sanders

Daniel Simmons, Sr.

Sharonda Singleton

Myra Thompson

We're **angry!** How can we help but be angry? This is horrible! Another mass shooting in the United States. Another act of terrorism by a white supremacist against black people. We're horrified.

The thing is, though, that we can turn away. A week from now this will be old news, and while we won't forget it, we'll be able to turn away from it because, really, it's so unpleasant, and really, it's not our problem.

But as much as, really, I'd like to do that, I have to recognize that turning away from this act of terror in Charleston's Emmanuel AME Church is sin.

I'm not talking about "personal" sin here. My personal sinfulness—greed, avarice, wrath, pride—any of the seven deadlies or others. This is not about my personal sinfulness; it's about my participation in *corporate* sin.

Corporate sin—sin of the corpus, the body, the community—is sinfulness that I participate in because I am part of the corpus. Whether I'm aware of it or not, whether I recognize it or not, I participate in this sinfulness because I participate in a society that is tainted by it.

Here's an example: When I decide what to buy based mostly on its cost, it's very likely that I am inadvertently supporting sweatshops around the world. When I buy a wonderfully inexpensive pair of jeans or sweater, it's probably because it was made by people working 16 hours a day for almost nothing, and I am complicit.

When the fish I eat was pulled from the ocean by men who are imprisoned on boats and forced to work at the point of a gun, that's slavery. That's corporate sin. And because I benefit—even unknowingly—from the slavery of those fishermen, I am complicit in it.

Racism in this country is also corporate sin.

We may not think of ourselves as personally prejudiced. I hope and trust that you are not someone who tells derogatory jokes or uses offensive language about people of other races.

We speak and sing week after week in this church about everyone being a child of God, about seeing the face of Jesus in everyone we meet, about loving our neighbors—all of our neighbors. I'm hoping and trusting that you take all that "Jesus stuff" seriously.

But regardless of whether we individually are racist, we are part of a culture that is racist. Some people call it "America's original sin." It's so pervasive that most of the time we don't even notice it.

Being white in this country means we benefit. We're far less likely to be stopped or ticketed when driving. We're far more likely to have had parents and grandparents who weren't "red-lined" and thus able to own homes in areas where the schools were good and the crime rate low—and because they earned equity on those homes, they were in many cases able to help us do the same. We're far more likely to have had family or school connections with people who helped us find jobs.

Most of the time we don't notice these things. Almost everyone we know is in the same situation, after all. It's "the norm."

But it's not the norm for black people in this country.

There are other examples.

When a young black man kills or rampages, our media calls him a thug. When a Muslim man kills or rampages, he is labeled a terrorist. When a white man kills or rampages, we call him a mentally ill loner.

Do you see what that difference in labeling does? A thug or a terrorist is an "other." He is dangerous—to be feared and punished. Someone who is mentally ill is to be pitied, to be cared for.

And that is sin. Different norms for different groups of people is not what Jesus came to teach. What was Paul's theme? "In Christ there is no Jew nor Greek, no slave nor free, no male and female." We are all one in Christ Jesus.

I'm hearing from black friends around the country, many of them saying that they're feeling numb. And terrified. Like the disciples in the ship when the storm ranged around them, what my black friends and colleagues are experiencing is a very real danger. Will they be shot in their church this morning? Will their teenaged son be the next to be killed for the crime of "walking while black"? Will their bikini-clad granddaughter be thrown to the ground and restrained there by a police officer who assumes she doesn't belong at the swimming pool?

When the disciples were terrified in their boat, as the waves swamped over the sides and the wind battered, they cried out to Jesus, who was sleeping in the stern. "Teacher, do you not care that we are perishing?" And Jesus woke up. He rebuked the wind, and said to the sea, "Peace! Be still!" Then the wind ceased, and there was calm.

The disciples thought they were perishing. But then Jesus made everything all right.

When we think we are perishing—when we're up against powers that are greater than we are—our faith reminds us that Jesus is in the boat with us. And Jesus cares. Jesus loves.

Sometimes Jesus cares and loves <u>through us</u>. We are Christians—Christ followers—the Body of Christ—the hands and feet of Jesus. We are called to repent of our sin and turn a different way.

Jesus calls us to repent of our complicity in corporate sin, whether it's the sin of forced labor/slavery, the sin of racism, the sin of dishonoring the earth, or the sin of turning away from these things because they're just too hard, too unpleasant. We might start, every Sunday when we pray the prayer of corporate confession during worship, by remembering and asking God's forgiveness for our participation in these sins.

Jesus calls us to repent, to go in a different direction, when it comes to the corporate sin of racism. Perhaps simply to speak up when those around us are explicitly racist. Not to sit quietly when Uncle Harry tells another racist joke or when Aunt Matilda Sue talks about the "glory days" of the Confederacy when her ancestors held human beings as property. Or when the guy we work with complains about how "those people" are taking away our "rights" to hold all the power in this country. Or the woman down the street worries that the "thugs" in Baltimore will contaminate her neighborhood.

This young man who thought it was his duty to kill black people and wanted to start a race war—he did not arrive at his racism in a vacuum. We speak of American

Muslims being "radicalized" by Islamic extremists. Who radicalized this young white supremacist? How did this kind of belief become "right" for him?

He was a member of a Lutheran church. Why weren't there enough Christian people there speaking up enough to counteract the racist attitudes he was learning?

There are many things we can do to stand up against the corporate sin of racism. To begin with, though, we will need five smooth stones. That's what Presbyterian pastor Thom Shuman wrote this week, saying that what we are <u>not</u> called to is hate.

> It would be easy to put on that heavy
> armor of anger,
> to slip our feet into the shoes of
> vengeance,
> to pick up our own weapons, and rush
> into battle.

Instead, he says, "we are called to a more difficult task."

> To set aside the armor,
> to lay down the weapons,
> to reach deep down inside our hearts and
> our souls
> where they have been placed so long ago
> and pull out those five smooth stones—
> compassion, inclusion, love, goodness,
> and forgiveness. [7]

Compassion, inclusion, love, goodness, and forgiveness.

---

[7] Thom M. Shuman, "Five Smooth Stones." Facebook. June 18, 2015.

You may have a slightly different list. In a little while two newly elected elders in this church will promise to serve this congregation "with energy, intelligence, imagination, and love." That's a good list. Maybe your smooth stones include peacefulness and justice, respect and welcome. Surely they all include love. And prayer.

And so let us pray.

Lord, we know that you care. We trust that your love for all of your children is more powerful than our hatred. Help us to recognize our participation in corporate sin, and forgive us, we pray. And guide us to dig into our hearts and souls to pull out those five smooth stones—the stones you planted there, the stones washed smooth by your love—so that we can stand up for your righteousness and justice.

And when we are afraid for ourselves, when racial tensions and religious tensions and political tensions threaten to overwhelm our boats, give us your smooth stones of peace and of trust.

Amen.

The Rev. Jeanne Gay *is currently Interim Pastor at Northminster Presbyterian Church; this sermon was preached when she served as Interim Pastor at Havenwood Presbyterian Church, a church of about 225 members in Lutherville, MD, in Baltimore County, just north of the city.*

A Peculiar Instinct

Robert Hoch

"Jerusalem, Jerusalem, the city that kills the prophets and stones those who are sent to it! How often have I desired to gather your children together as a hen gathers her brood under her wings, and you were not willing! See, your house is left to you, desolate. For I tell you, you will not see me again until you say, 'Blessed is the one who comes in the name of the Lord.'" Matthew 23:37-39

What then are we to say about these things? If God is for us, who is against us? He who did not withhold his own Son, but gave him up for all of us, will he not with him also give us everything else? Who will bring any charge against God's elect? It is God who justifies. Who is to condemn? It is Christ Jesus, who died, yes, who was raised, who is at the right hand of God, who indeed intercedes for us. Who will separate us from the love of Christ? Will hardship, or distress, or persecution, or famine, or nakedness, or peril, or sword? As it is written,

"For your sake we are being killed all day long;
   we are accounted as sheep to be slaughtered."

No, in all these things we are more than conquerors through him who loved us. For I am convinced that neither death, nor life, nor angels, nor rulers, nor things present, nor things to come, nor powers, nor height, nor depth, nor anything else in all creation, will be able to separate us from the love of God in Christ Jesus our Lord. Romans 8:31-39

Yesterday afternoon, I was alone with our two year old, trapped in the house because of the bad weather we've been seeing. But when the weather broke, I took her on a walk to a park not far from our house. On the way over, I looked ahead of us to see a baby bird, an apparently dead chick on the sidewalk, probably blown out of its nest by the blustery weather. This is always a sad sight, and I was glad that our two-year-old had not noticed. But then there was something different, and it took me a moment to see what I was seeing, something right and wrong at the same time: the mother of the bird was brooding on top of its chick, her wings covering it, as if the baby were still in her nest, trying to keep it warm, even though it had evidently died.

As I approached, the mother robin crouched further, watching me, and finally succumbed to nature and instinct, flying away. When I came back, twenty minutes later, the mother robin had not returned.

I share this image with you because it strikes me that the nine who were killed in the Charleston AME Church are the church's daughters and sons, our own kin. Stricken by racism, shattered by gun shots, tossed to the ground, bodies deformed by savagery inspired by stupidity and ignorance—they may seem far from us, but in fact, we are kin to them and they to us through baptism. In a sense, this church, your congregation, is just one part of a much larger movement, a movement that gathered them as it has gathered us.

But I am afraid that sometimes an ordinary robin has more motherly instinct than we do. It would be too easy to abandon the dead, to forget them, or to imagine that this is somehow so far removed from our lives as people of the church, that it does not impinge on us, not on us personally, or to let this news run its natural and inevitable course, finally exhausting itself in meaninglessness.

Even so, that robin knew her chick and would not abandon it. And perhaps now is our time to grieve over the lost children of the Charleston Church. To, if you will, return for a moment to the lives the church birthed and nurtured through baptism.

What more can be said? What word will satisfy or offer healing to the wound? After so many tragedies, Ferguson, Baltimore, New York, Sandy Hook, movie theaters in Colorado ... at a certain point, what can you say? what can you say that will make a difference? Personally, I have felt numb following the news breaking on Thursday morning.

Numb and no words. But as I thought about that mother robin and her baby chick, it occurred to me that this creature was, also, similarly in a place she never imagined herself: sitting on a sidewalk, exposed to predators. Yet it was the most natural place for her to be at that moment, doing what instinct demanded of her.

Our own action on this occasion might not be so self-evident. But it strikes me that each of us was baptized in the church. And during our baptism, the congregation pledged to pray for us, to be our friend, to support us, to be Christ to us.

Nine people were shot during a Wednesday night Bible Study, in the AME Church of Charleston.

My sense of instinct, or what's left of it, leads me to think that today we ought to remember the baptism of those nine and, in so doing, remember our own baptism, the baptism that welcomed us into the life of the church. With that in mind, I am going to repeat the name of each of the nine who were killed, embodying in words and action the baptismal sacrament that forms us as a community.

But I can't do this alone. [Move to the baptismal font and, during the congregational response, dip hand into the water, to visually remember their baptism.] Baptism is enacted by the whole church, through the activity of the Spirit. So, if you would, after each name, respond as a congregation, remembering the baptisms of the deceased of the AME Church in Charleston, saying " ... baptized in the name of the Father, and the Son, and the Holy Spirit."

Cynthia Hurd, 54 years old, daughter of God, child of the covenant ...
baptized in the name of the Father, and the Son, and the Holy Spirit.

Susie Jackson, 87 years old, daughter of God, child of the covenant ...
baptized in the name of the Father, and the Son, and the Holy Spirit.

Ethel Lance, 70 years old, daughter of God, child of the covenant ...
baptized in the name of the Father, and the Son, and the Holy Spirit.

DePayne Middleton Doctor, 49 years old, daughter of God, child of the covenant ...
baptized in the name of the Father, and the Son, and the Holy Spirit.

Clementa Pinkney, 41 years old, son of God, child of the covenant ...
baptized in the name of the Father, and the Son, and the Holy Spirit.

Tywanza Sanders, 26 years old, daughter of God, child of the covenant ...

> **baptized in the name of the Father, and the Son, and the Holy Spirit.**

Daniel Simmons, 72 years old, son of God, child of the covenant ...

> **baptized in the name of the Father, and the Son, and the Holy Spirit.**

Sharonda Singleton, 45 years old, daughter of God, child of the covenant ...

> **baptized in the name of the Father, and the Son, and the Holy Spirit.**

Myra Thompson, 59 years old, daughter of God, child of the covenant ...

> **baptized in the name of the Father, and the Son, and the Holy Spirit.**

> > *Lord, we commend to you these your sons and daughters, sheep of your own fold, sinners of your own redeeming. Receive them as a mother rejoices for her children, as a father welcomes the prodigal home. Receive them as one day you will receive us. Amen.*[8]

Their baptism is completed in death.

But our baptism, until that final day, requires improvement, and this leads us inevitably to Dylann Roof, the shooter. On first glance, he does not seem to belong in this group except as the accused. And actually, instinct would like to keep him as far from his victims as possible. A US Senator from South Carolina called Roof a "monster" and something other than human. Roof's uncle says he would be happy to throw the switch on him, administering

---

[8] Adapted from "Commendation Prayer" in the *Book of Common Worship: Pastoral Edition* (Louisville: Westminster/John Knox Press, 1993), 209.

the execution of his nephew by his own hand.⁹ It's very easy, I think, to make him into a monster: what he did was monstrous.

And yet ... he is still ours, our kin, baptized with the baptism we are baptized. From what I understand, he is a member of the Evangelical Lutheran Church, on their rolls, and thus he, like his victims, shares this baptism.

There's an additional wrinkle to this story: Two of the people he killed on Wednesday received their theological education from a Lutheran Seminary.

Elizabeth Eaton, presiding bishop of the ELCA had this to say: "All of a sudden and for all of us, this is an intensely personal tragedy," she said. "One of our own is alleged to have shot and killed two who adopted us as their own."¹⁰

One of our own ...

Some members of his extended family are prepared to execute him, vow that they will show him no mercy.

Not too surprising, really. People said similar things about the Newtown school shooter, the boy who fatally shot 20 children and 6 adult staff. Or the Boston bombers. The police who attacked African American protesters in Ferguson called them "animals"—not human. Worthy of

---

⁹ Jeremy Borden, "For accused killer Dylann Roof, a life that had quietly drifted off track" in *The Washington Post* (18 June 2015), 19 April 2016 <https://www.washingtonpost.com/politics/accused-killer-in-sc-slayings-described-as-a-quiet-loner/2015/06/18/a4127390-15d0-11e5-89f3-61410da94eb1_story.html>

¹⁰ "ELCA Leader Expresses Grief Over Shooting in South Carolina" in Evangelical Lutheran Church in America (18 June 2015), accessed 19 April 2016 <http://elca.org/News-and-Events/7753>.

guns, tear gas, and beatings—or chokeholds—but not human.

> *Worthy of a lethal injection, but not prayer.*
>
> *Worthy of a gunshot, but not understanding.*
>
> *Worthy of a prison cell, but not community.*
>
> *Worthy of punishment, but not forgiveness.*

Which is, by the way, precisely what one of the daughters of Ethel Lance offered to Roof: "I will never be able to hold [my mother] again, but I forgive you, and have mercy on your soul. You hurt me. You hurt a lot of people but God forgives you, and I forgive you." Felicia Sanders—mother of victim Tywanza Sanders and a survivor of the church shooting herself—said, "Every fiber in my body hurts, and I will never be the same." "As we said in the Bible study, we enjoyed you," she said of Roof. "But may God have mercy on you."[11]

Someone said it was too soon to forgive. I'm not sure I disagree: everything in me resists forgiveness. And it is precisely this that should awaken us to something seemingly right and wrong at the same time: the people of the AME Church in Charleston refuse to act according to instinct, the instinct of anger, the instinct of deep and completely predictable hostility.

Somehow, they know what to do. Almost like instinct, but an instinct born of the Spirit, not merely flesh and blood. *It's surreal,* one of the family members said. Arthur Hurd, husband of Cynthia Hurd, said, "I would love to hate

---

[11] Bob Fredericks, "Shooting Victims Families Forgive Gunmen in Court" in the *New York Post* (19 June 2015) accessed 19 April 2016 <http://nypost.com/2015/06/19/some-forgive-massacre-suspect-at-first-court-appearance/>.

you, but hate's not in me. If I hate you I'm no better than you."[12]

And no different either. This is the danger we face: that we will come to reflect the very thing we fear.

Christ, we are told, casts out all fear. Christ also speaks of himself as a "mother hen" who longs to gather Jerusalem, the nation that kills its prophets, to himself. Love runs deep in Christ. God's love runs deeper than our violence. Christ's humanity runs deeper than our inhumanity. Christ was given the cross, but did not give us the same as we gave him. We dealt out death, but Christ poured out life and love and redemption.

We dealt out betrayal, leaving him to be devoured, but Christ says to us, "You are mine" and "I am with you always, even to the end of the age." Betrayal is not in him; death is not his way, but life; judgement belongs to him, but instead, he offers mercy and is, indeed, the mercy seat.

I don't know about you, but I'm not sure what to do with all that has happened in our country of late. But I am hoping that I still remember whose I am. Whose we are. That I have some shred of Christ still living and breathing in me.

I hope I have the wisdom of a mother robin, if only for a moment, if only for an hour. To be what I am called to be, perhaps in spite of myself, in spite of all reason, but because of the deep indwelling of Christ.

The Christ who joins us here, in this place. Far from heaven. Far from where we should be, what we should have been. Far from singing the song we were given to sing. But

---

[12] Ibid.

Christ is here. As he was fully on the Cross, so he is fully in our world of bloodshed and grief. As he is with the Charleston AME church that worships this morning. As he is with those who grieve the loss of loved ones.

As he is with Dylann Roof, 21 years old, son of God, child of the covenant ... baptized in the name of the Father, and the Son, and the Holy Spirit. Amen.

The Rev. Robert Hoch will become Pastor of First and Franklin Presbyterian Church, Baltimore, in June 2016; he previously served as Associate Professor of Homiletics and Worship at the University of Dubuque Theological Seminary. This sermon was preached at the yoked congregations of Scotch Grove and Center Junction, Iowa, following the mass shooting at the Emanuel AME Church of Charleston on June 17, 2015.

A Stronghold in Times of Trouble

Roger Scott Powers

The Lord is a stronghold for the oppressed,
   a stronghold in times of trouble.
And those who know your name put their trust in you,
   for you, O Lord, have not forsaken those who seek you.
Sing praises to the Lord, who dwells in Zion.
   Declare his deeds among the peoples.
For he who avenges blood is mindful of them;
   he does not forget the cry of the afflicted.
Be gracious to me, O Lord.
   See what I suffer from those who hate me;
   you are the one who lifts me up from the gates of death,
so that I may recount all your praises,
   and, in the gates of daughter Zion,
   rejoice in your deliverance.
The nations have sunk in the pit that they made;
   in the net that they hid has their own foot been caught.
The Lord has made himself known, he has executed judgement;
   the wicked are snared in the work of their own hands.
The wicked shall depart to Sheol,
   all the nations that forget God.
For the needy shall not always be forgotten,
   nor the hope of the poor perish for ever.
Rise up, O Lord! Do not let mortals prevail;
   let the nations be judged before you.
Put them in fear, O Lord;
   let the nations know that they are only human.
Psalm 9:9-20

On Thursday morning, we woke up, as did the rest of the nation, to the horrific news coming out of Charleston, South Carolina. Nine people had been shot and killed during a Wednesday night Bible study at a historic black church, Emanuel African Methodist Episcopal, the oldest A.M.E. church in the South. The gunman, a young white man, had sat with them in the Bible study for an hour before he pulled out his handgun and opened fire.

His nine victims—all of them African-American—included a mother of four, a recent college graduate, the sister of a former North Carolina lawmaker, and a politician who was also the church's pastor. They ranged in age from 26 to 87 years old.

- Clementa Pinckney, 41, was the church's pastor and had served as a Democratic senator in the state's General Assembly for 19 years.
- Tywanza Sanders, 26, called himself a poet, artist and businessman. He graduated last year from Allen University, in Columbia, S.C.
- DePayne Middleton-Doctor, 49, was an admissions coordinator at Southern Wesleyan University's Charleston learning center and mother to four daughters.
- Cynthia Hurd, 54, worked as a librarian for 31 years and was the sister of former state Sen. Malcolm Graham.
- Sharonda Coleman-Singleton, 45, a mother of three, was a part-time minister at Emanuel AME Church and worked as a speech pathologist at Goose Creek High School.
- Susie Jackson, 87, was a longtime member of Emanuel AME Church and sang in the choir.

- Ethel Lance, 70, raised five children and worked as a custodian at the church for about 30 years, but on Wednesday was there as a member.
- Daniel L. Simmons, Sr., 74, was a member of the ministerial staff at Emanuel AME Church.
- Myra Thompson, 59, was another pastor at the church.

With millions of people all across our nation, we mourn their tragic deaths.

Later on Thursday, police arrested their principal suspect, 21-year-old Dylann Roof, more than two hundred miles away in Shelby, North Carolina. They returned him to South Carolina in shackles where he was charged with nine counts of murder and one firearm charge. In addition, the Justice Department, the FBI, and the U.S. Attorney's Office are investigating the shooting as a hate crime as well as a possible act of domestic terrorism.

After I had taken in this terrible news, I looked at the lectionary readings for today and found in Psalm 9 a prayer of lament that was amazingly relevant to the moment, as if the victims and their families were themselves declaring their unflagging faith in God even in the face of such a monstrous crime. Listen to the words of the Psalmist:

> *The Lord is a stronghold for the oppressed,*
>   *a stronghold in times of trouble. ...*
>
> *Be gracious to me, O Lord.*
>   *See what I suffer from those who hate me;*
>   *you are the one who lifts me up from the gates of death,*
> *so that I may recount all your praises,*
>   *and, in the gates of daughter Zion,*
>   *rejoice in your deliverance.*

> *The Lord has made himself known, he has executed judgment;*
>> *the wicked are snared in the work of their own hands.*

For many, a mass shooting of people attending a Bible study inside a church would be cause for questioning their faith in God. After all, a church is supposed to be a place of refuge and safety. But for the families of the victims at Emanuel AME Church, this tragedy drew them closer to God. They know that the first heart to break last Wednesday night was God's, and that God is supporting them and upholding them in their grief and sorrow. Indeed, the very name of their church, Emanuel, means "God is with us." For them, as for the Psalmist, "The Lord ... is a stronghold in times of trouble."

I don't know how many of you saw the reports from the bond hearing on Friday. The families of the victims showed their unwavering faith in a God of love as one by one they expressed their pain and sorrow to Dylann Roof and then offered him their forgiveness. They urged him to repent, to confess his sins and turn to God. Nadine Collier, the daughter of 70-year-old victim Ethel Lance said: "You took something very precious away from me. I will never talk to her ever again. I will never be able to hold her again. But I forgive you. And have mercy on your soul. You hurt me. You hurt a lot of people but God forgive you, and I forgive you." Felicia Sanders—mother of 26-year-old victim Tywanza Sanders and a survivor of the church shooting—said: "We welcomed you Wednesday night in our Bible study with open arms. ... You have killed some of the most beautifulest people that I know. Every fiber in my body hurts, and I will never be the same. ... As we said in the Bible study, we enjoyed you, but may God have mercy on you."[13] Even in the face of such a monstrous crime, they found it within themselves to communicate Jesus' message of love and forgiveness. They knew, with Dr. King, that "darkness cannot drive out darkness: only light can do that. Hate cannot drive out hate: only love can do that."[14]

Whenever tragedies like this one in Charleston occur, we search for explanations. We want to know why it happened. Some point to the easy availability of guns in our country, as President Obama did in his statement this week. He said that "once again, innocent people were killed in part because someone who wanted to inflict harm had no trouble getting their hands on a gun. ... At some point, we as a country will have to reckon with the fact that this type of mass violence does not happen in other advanced countries. It doesn't happen in other places with this kind of frequency. And it is in our power to do something about it. I say that recognizing the politics in this town foreclose a lot of those avenues right now. But it would be wrong for us not to acknowledge it. And at some point, it's going to be important for the American people to come to grips with it, and for us to be able to shift how we think about the issue of gun violence collectively."[15]

---

[13] Nikita Steward and Richard Pérez-Peña, "In Charleston, Raw Emotion at Hearing for Suspect in Church Shooting," *New York Times*, June 19, 2015; "Dylan Roof Bond Hearing. Victims Address Charleston Shooter In Court," *YouTube* video, 6:58, June 19, 2015, <https://www.youtube.com/watch?v=e26Eysq22Y>

[14] Martin Luther King, Jr., *Strength to Love* (Philadelphia: Fortress Press, 1963), 51.

[15] Barack Obama, "Statement by the President on the Shooting in Charleston, South Carolina" (speech, Washington, DC, June 18, 2015) <https://www.whitehouse.gov/the-press-

Some say that the shooter must be mentally ill, thus further stigmatizing those who suffer with mental health issues. But isn't it interesting that when people of color commit acts of violence, the media have no trouble believing that they were in their right minds and knew what they were doing, labeling them as "thugs" or "terrorists." But when white people commit acts of violence, the media jump to the conclusion that they must be mentally ill, as if to say that no white person in their right mind would do such a thing! It's just one of many examples of racial bias in our society.

From what we know so far, it seems clear that the Charleston shooting was a racially motivated crime. Survivors of the shooting say that Dylann Roof made racist statements as he gunned down his victims. His Facebook page shows a photo of him wearing a jacket with the patches of apartheid South Africa and the formerly white-ruled African country of Rhodesia. And his website includes a 2,000-word manifesto in which he identifies himself as a white nationalist and says he was "truly awakened" to his beliefs after reading what he found on the website of a racist hate group called the Council of Conservative Citizens. The manifesto concludes with a section labeled "An Explanation." "I have no choice," it reads. "I am not in the position to, alone, go into the ghetto and fight. I chose Charleston because it is [the] most historic city in my state, and at one time had the highest ratio of blacks to Whites in the country. We have no skinheads, no real KKK, no one doing anything but talking on the internet. Well someone

---

office/2015/06/18/statement-president-shooting-charleston-south-carolina>

has to have the bravery to take it to the real world, and I guess that has to be me."[16]

This points to the larger problem of racism and white supremacy on which our country was built and that still pervades our society today. President Obama alluded to this when he quoted what Dr. King had to say just over 50 years ago after four little girls were killed in the bombing of a black church in Birmingham, Alabama. "They say to each of us, black and white alike, that ... we must be concerned not merely about who murdered them, but about the system, the way of life, the philosophy which produced the murderers."[17]

White supremacist groups that spew racial hatred, such as the one that influenced Dylann Roof, are only the most extreme example of the problem of white supremacy in the United States. White supremacy remains a part of our culture. We see it in police brutality against African Americans in our cities. We see it in racial profiling. We see it in disproportionately higher unemployment rates and incarceration rates for people of color as compared to whites. We see it in our attitudes toward the predominantly black, poverty-stricken neighborhoods of East and West Baltimore. We see it every time a school teacher acts as if a white child has more potential than a black child.

---

[16] Brendan O'Connor, "Here Is What Appears to Be Dylann Roof's Racist Manifesto," June 20, 2015, <http://gawker.com/here-is-what-appears-to-be-dylann-roofs-racist-manifest-1712767241>

[17] Barack Obama, "Statement by the President on the Shooting in Charleston, South Carolina" (speech, Washington, DC, June 18, 2015) <https://www.whitehouse.gov/the-press-office/2015/06/18/statement-president-shooting-charleston-south-carolina>

As Abbi Heimach, a seminarian and leader in the Presbyterian Peace Fellowship, wrote: "Our country's history of slavery and genocide continues to shape all of us today, imposing trauma and violence upon people of color's bodies and nurturing internalized superiority in white people. Knowing that all of us are dehumanized in this reign of white supremacy, we pray for God to empower each of us to tear down this idol and declare God's reign in the struggle for freedom."[18]

We need to realize that, like Jesus and his disciples on the Sea of Galilee, we are all in the same boat. What hurts one of us hurts all of us. And when we find ourselves in the midst of a storm, buffeted by headwinds of hatred, we need to work together with love if we are going to get through the storm together.

Most importantly, God is present with us in Jesus Christ. God is "a stronghold in times of trouble." God cares for us. God supports and upholds us. And through Jesus Christ, God saves us, because we cannot save ourselves.

It is when we come up against our own limitations that we most often reach out to God. We feel a need for a power outside of ourselves to support and sustain us. And God is present with us in Jesus Christ offering us that support and love. Faith can give us courage in the most trying of circumstances, knowing that wherever we are, whatever we

---

[18] Abbi Heimach, on behalf of the National Committee of the Presbyterian Peace Fellowship, "Pastoral Response Letter to Charleston," June 20, 2015
<http://presbypeacefellowship.org/content/pastoral-response-letter-charleston#.VtmV7rQllYY>

are doing, no matter how alone we may feel, we are always in God's care. Thanks be to God. Amen.

The Rev. Roger Scott Powers serves as Pastor at Light Street Presbyterian Church, a congregation of about 50 near the Inner Harbor in downtown Baltimore. He is a former Moderator of the Presbytery of Baltimore.

Things that Make for Peace

Brandon Frick

Let me hear what God the Lord will speak,
  for he will speak peace to his people,
  to his faithful, to those who turn to him in their hearts.
Surely his salvation is at hand for those who fear him,
  that his glory may dwell in our land.
Steadfast love and faithfulness will meet;
  righteousness and peace will kiss each other.
Faithfulness will spring up from the ground,
  and righteousness will look down from the sky.
The Lord will give what is good,
  and our land will yield its increase.
Righteousness will go before him,
  and will make a path for his steps.

Psalm 85:8-13

As he came near and saw the city, he wept over it, saying, 'If you, even you, had only recognized on this day the things that make for peace! But now they are hidden from your eyes. Indeed, the days will come upon you, when your enemies will set up ramparts around you and surround you, and hem you in on every side. They will crush you to the ground, you and your children within you, and they will not leave within you one stone upon another; because you did not recognize the time of your visitation from God. Luke 19:41-44

As Jesus draws ever closer to Jerusalem and ever closer to his own death and resurrection, he weeps—not for himself, but for this royal city, the city of David. He laments the inability of its inhabitants to see the things that make for peace and God's very presence among them. In that city, Jew and Gentile lived alongside one another, with the Roman government in control and its Jewish residents permitted to practice their religion and customs. Though it originally entered Jerusalem as a hostile, invading force, Rome made a promise to provide *pax et securitas*, peace and security, to all of its conquered lands. Though defeated, Jerusalem would be defended by the mightiest army that the world had ever known.

There was "peace" in Jerusalem if by that we mean the absence of war. But, that's not what Jesus, a first-century Palestinian Jew, would have meant when he lamented the absence of peace. The word for peace is *shalom*, but to encompass the richness of this term, we might better think of it as wholeness. A life marked by *shalom* is one that fully embraces the truth of our creation: that we belong wholly to God and were made to live in right relationship with one another. *Shalom* is rooted in the truth that we are all children of God, bound together in that family with and for one another.

Shalom, wholeness, was largely absent in first-century Jerusalem where the divisions between Jew and Gentile, slave and free, male and female, rich and poor were so deeply ingrained in the culture that they didn't have to be enforced; they were assumed and promoted by many in the city who could not see, as Jesus says, "the things that make for peace." There was only power used to hold each of the fragmented parts of Roman society in its proper place. In 70 A.D Jewish Zealots attempted to overthrow Roman rule, and in trying to break out of this strict boundary, Jerusalem's "peace" was exposed as a lie. The rebellion was crushed. Jewish Historian Josephus was outside of the city when the Roman forces broke through and leveled the city so that "there was left nothing to make those that came after believe Jerusalem had ever been inhabited."[19] All but the Western wall of the temple was destroyed, and generations of Jews living in Jerusalem met their end in that siege.

Though they were besieged, their foes did not come from outside, but inside. Overnight, neighbor became enemy. Because when a place substitutes power for wholeness, this thing that merely looks like peace, that only looks like a unified whole, begins to crack, even if ever so slightly. And over time deep fissures begin to form where there were once only delicate cracks. And from those deep, broken places arise those who are themselves already broken and committed to destruction.

And so Jesus laments. As the Creator of this place, the Bringer of true Peace and the Savior of people, he weeps for a people who cannot see the beauty of the wholeness God has prepared for them. We repeatedly encounter individuals weeping in Luke's gospel, and their tears and wailing are always the result of those they love who have either already died or are soon to die. The only other time Jesus is said to "weep" in the gospels is in John where he is overcome at Lazarus' death. Although our English translations say that he "weeps" in both situations, the Greek indicates that he cries silently at Lazarus' death, while he wails at the sight of false peace that will soon destroy Jerusalem. Though Lazarus was already dead, it is Jerusalem, slowly dying from the inside, that overwhelms the Healer of the Nations.

---

[19] Josephus, *Of the War, Book VII, Chapter 1*

I have to wonder if Jesus Christ is not weeping over Charleston. And not just because nine brothers and sisters in Christ lost their lives at the hands of a 21-year-old after studying scripture together, but because like Jerusalem, the "peace" in Charleston and places like it is not one dedicated to creating wholeness for individuals or communities, but simply to holding unconnected pieces together.

By now, I'm sure the vast majority of you know I spent the first 24 years of my life in South Carolina, but the Frick family has a much longer history there. In 1754 Johann Thomas Frick sailed aboard the vessel Priscilla with his family into Charleston harbor and settled 125 miles northwest of Charleston. Still to this day you will find numerous descendants of Thomas Frick living within miles of the 250-acre bounty he was deeded. The story of my family—my story—cannot be told without South Carolina, without its lakes, its pine trees, its red clay and most importantly its people. But South Carolina is not merely the setting in which my story takes place; it's a significant character in that story that has had no less hand in forming who I am than my family and closest friends.

And so this week I have grieved the loss of nine fellow Christians. I have grieved for Dylann Roof, his family and friends. And I have grieved for South Carolina, not only for its loss and pain, but because like Jerusalem, it has mistaken the absence of hostility for a *shalom* that heals and makes people, families, churches and towns whole.

From what I gather, Dylann and I grew up just miles from one another, he at While Knoll High and I at Chapin High. We both grew up Lutheran, he at St. Paul's and I at St. Peter's. When I see Dylann Roof, I see an immensely troubled young man, but I also see a guy who I could have played games with as a child or sat in classes with as a teenager, and so I wonder, despite our age difference, if we might not share some of the same experiences.

If Dylann Roof was anything like me, he grew up in a place where there were white neighborhoods and black neighborhoods maintained by strict, though unspoken, boundaries. If he was anything like me, he was familiar with a variety of racial stereotypes and slurs by the time he graduated high school. If he was anything like me, he grew up seeing the Confederate flag on coffee mugs, key chains, coffee mugs, t-shirts, hats, printed on the back window of pickup trucks and yes, flying over some of his neighbors' homes and the state capitol down the road. And, if he was anything like me, when he was 14, he flew one of those flags in his bedroom right over the nightstand where he kept his Bible, and he told anyone he met about the flag keeping alive the memory of soldiers fighting for the homeland: that it represented states' rights and heritage, not hate.

If he was anything like me, he was surrounded by, and was a proponent of, things that do not make for peace, and yet he truly believed that the world in which he lived was marked by the kind of wholeness Jesus so desired for Jerusalem.

Now, I need to be careful here because I don't want to suggest that Dylann Roof is the inevitable product of that culture. My life and others serve as a witness to a different outcome. We probably won't ever know all the factors that came together to lead him to Mother Emanuel 10 days ago, but that question must lead South Carolina to ask hard questions about the difference between a false and true peace.

There is a new state of affairs in South Carolina. State Representative Doug Brannon, who has been vocal in the call to take down the Confederate Flag since his friend Clemente Pinckney was killed leading Bible Study, captured this change in a recent interview. He was asked about how he viewed the Confederate Flag flying on state house grounds before and after the shooting. He said, "I walked past it on a semi-regular basis, but I don't look at it. That may sound ridiculous, but I don't look at it. So, it didn't mean anything to me. ...When I see it now, I see it on a license plate on the front of a car driving to a church where nine people died."[20] These things were once, as Jesus says in our text, "hidden" from his eyes, but have now been exposed as things that will keep South Carolina, so marked by its historical racial divide, from ever being made whole.

But this is not a reality only for South Carolina. We deceive ourselves and the truth is not in us if we view the issues of race as unique to them. Charleston is not the only place in the world clinging hopelessly to this false peace. McKinney, Ferguson, Cleveland, New York City, and of course, Baltimore: it seems like we are reminded far too frequently of the deep wounds that still exist in our country around issues of race. But, again, we deceive ourselves if we think that race is the only thing upon which we try to patch together a passable peace. There are too many people that walk through our church doors on a daily basis seeking wholeness for us to believe that lie. Too many of our neighbors looking for help paying their rent, or to keep their lights on by no fault of their own; too many searching for a safe place far away from dangerous homes; too many trying to figure out how to make peace with those they've harmed

---

[20] Doug Brannon, S.C. State Legislator Hopes To Remove Confederate Flag This Summer. All Things Considered/NPR. Web. 26 June 2015. <http://www.npr.org/2015/06/22/416538096/s-c-state-legislator-i-think-well-take-down-the-flag-this-summer>.

and dealing with the shame and confusion that comes with it. So, the tragedy that took place at Mother Emanuel must force us all to open our eyes to the things in this world and in our lives that only have the appearance of peace and to see the places within ourselves, in our homes, our relationships, in our neighborhoods where there are only fragments tenuously holding together.

Psalm 85: 8-13 is beautiful not only in form but in content. It describes a world in which creation flourishes; a world in which paths of righteousness and justice are clearly marked out; a world in which steadfastness love, faithfulness and peace are found in our streets, homes, and in our hearts and minds. The imagery here so clearly describes God's desires for our world, but, if we're honest with ourselves, it describes a world that seems so far-removed from the blood-stained floors of Emanuel Church that we scoff at the possibility it could ever exist. It can seem hardly worth the hard questions we'll have to ask, the stark answers we'll have to come to terms with, the need for repentance that will almost inevitably ensue, and the ongoing work of reconciliation to which we will have to commit ourselves.

But I want to tell why I think that world will exist. It's not because I'm a young idealist or wish for utopia. It's because I have seen the in-breaking of the world described in Psalm 85 in our own world. I remember, even as a teenager, what it was like to have my eyes opened to the things that make for peace, and the knowledge that it was time to pull that flag down off my bedroom wall, to admit the error of hanging it and to have some difficult, but necessary, conversations with folks who I had earlier tried to convert to the "Lost Cause." But, even more recently I've seen it break in through the families of the Charleston Nine who spoke at Dylann Roof's deposition hearing. Nadine Collier, whose 70-year-old mother, Ethel Lance, was killed, told Dylann, "You took something very precious away from me. ... I will never talk to her ever again. I will never be able to hold her again. But I forgive you. And have mercy on your soul." Anthony Thompson, whose mother Myra was killed, told Dylann, "I would just like you to know that I forgive you and my family forgives you. But we would like you to take this opportunity to repent. Repent, confess, give your life to the one that matters the most—Christ—so he can change it, change your ways no matter what happened to you." Their ability to forgive seems as unlikely as the world described in Psalm 85, and yet I know it's happened. Those who most acutely know what Dylann Roof took that day also know the kind of peace Jesus is talking about: one built on eyes opened to the things that do not make for peace, one that acknowledges the need for repentance from those things, and one that serves for the church as a profound reminder that it is Jesus Christ who empowers this kind of peace.

I know that world will come because Jesus Christ is in the business of binding up the broken people and places of this world and making them whole as individuals and communities. Entering Jerusalem, he wept; but he didn't stop there. He kept living the kind of life that could reconcile us with ourselves, one another and with God even though it would take him to the cross. When Lazarus died, Jesus wept; but he didn't stop there. He called him out of the tomb and into the freedom of new life. And because he is our Risen, Living Lord, he continues to lament our inability to see the things that make for peace in our homes, our neighborhoods and in places like Charleston; but he doesn't stop there. He makes us whole by opening our eyes to his presence and showing us, sometimes through a revelatory moment that strikes at our conscience, sometimes through state legislators, and sometimes through the witness of mourning, the things that make for peace. The state motto of South Carolina is Dum Spiro Spero, "While I breathe, I hope"—and when I am confronted by mercy and power of Jesus Christ, I can do no other.

The Rev. Brandon Frick is Associate Pastor at Woods Memorial Presbyterian Church, a large suburban congregation of 2125 members in Severna Park, MD, southeast of Baltimore near Annapolis, MD.

SECTION III:
Looking to the Future

Let the Boys Live

Keith O. Page

Then the king of Egypt spoke to Shiphrah and Puah, the two midwives who helped the Hebrew women. "When you help the Hebrew women give birth," he said to them. "kill the baby if it is a boy, but if it is a girl, let it live. But the midwives were God-fearing and so did not obey the king; instead, they let the boys live. Exodus 1:15-18

When Herod realized that the visitors from the East had tricked, he was furious. He gave orders to kill all the boys in Bethlehem and its neighborhood who were two years old and younger-this was done in accordance with what he had learned from the visitors about the time when the star had appeared. Matthew 2:16

Our Old Testament lesson seems to sparkle with a painful reality that would cause us to believe that history is indeed cyclical. The Hebrew people are growing in number and in strength, much to the fear of the established North African Egyptians. The Hebrew people's numbers and abilities appear to suggest the ability to defeat their Egyptian taskmasters, rendering the Egyptians powerless. The great temptation for Pharaoh here is to turn assumption into fact and begin a campaign of fear mongering designed not only to manipulate the emotions of the masses, but to turn the energies of possible reconciliation into the violent defense of an outdated ideal. As we look at this familiar text, we must lay aside the traps of temptation set by the storytellers to demonize the Egyptians. The book of Genesis tells us that we are all God's children, and they are certainly no exception. We must also not get caught up with the storyteller Cecil B. DeMille when we consider the ethnicities of the characters in the drama. Despite our familiar images, Egypt is in North Africa, and Africans have had slaves for thousands of years. Regardless of being oppressed or oppressor, we are all God's children.

This text chills us because we know that Pharaoh's hatred and fear are very much alive. That fear drives a state and federal justice system to incarcerate more African American men than any other racial group. Our prisons are overcrowded with our African American men, and that fear driven system would rather build more prisons than seek rehabilitation for our current prison population. However, the prison system is simply the poster child for a much larger problem. The breakdown of the African American family extends all the way to the separation of slave families because the males commanded higher prices. The larger problem in our society is that many of us as human beings see differences in appearance as differences in value. We also see "the different one" as a threat to be subdued rather than as a friend to be embraced.

Our news networks have short reporting cycles and short attention spans. Freddy Gray is not an isolated incident. Does anyone remember Rodney King, the motorist who was violently beaten by a gang of law enforcement officers? Do I need to call the roll: Shawn Bell, Amadou Diallo, Michael Brown or Deborah Bland?

It seems that Pharaoh is far from dead. Freddy Gray is dead, and shockwaves continue to reverberate across the country. Men, women and children are seeing their anger reach a boiling point spilling over into violent rage and mass destruction. Businesses are looted and cars destroyed as a mass of God's children with one voice cry out: Enough! Moreover, we see law enforcement officials treating the residents of our city as enemies of the state. The privileges and opportunities that some have to make a better life now clash with the shattered dreams and senseless violence of a marginalized and hopeless people. Yes, there are those who would use the chaotic violence as an avenue for personal advantage. They are simply the children of a capitalistic nation which sees and advertises any situation as an opportunity to either make money or to spend it.

Our New Testament focuses on another fearful leader acting in desperation. The slight difference in this text is that Herod believes the wise men's prophecies. What Pharaoh did not find out until the Red Sea, Herod already knew: that it was futile to fight against the Word of God. It is indeed fear, Pharaoh's fear, that leads the police to jail our young men. It is fear, Herod's fear, that drives a welfare system to give poor families enough money to survive but not enough to rise out of desperate circumstances. It is fear, Pharaoh's fear, that keeps drugs flowing in some neighborhoods and not in others. It is fear, Herod's fear, that will not keep guns off the street as long as African Americans are killing each other.

In the midst of this chaotic moment, how can we as the people of God respond? How can we bring comfort to the mothers who are powerless to shield their children from the drugs and violence? How can we bring Divine universal clarity to stereotyped division and complicated reaction?

How can we as individuals and as a church really make a positive difference amid the toxicity of polarized passions?

First, we are called to examine our own prejudices. God's children in all races, creeds and cultures do bad things. Why do some of us feel more fear when we are around African Americans (especially men) than Whites? We must also be aware of the ways that our society emphasizes the negativity of African American actions while downplaying the same actions by Whites. For example, the different penalties for crack cocaine users and powder cocaine users. This is true only because the users of crack cocaine are largely African American and the users of powder cocaine are disproportionately White. The Egyptian belief that Hebrew boys are any more dangerous than Egyptian boys is as bad as the arrest and mistreatment of our African American boys. Dispelling this lie begins with us in our conversations and interactions with the people around us.

Second, we must change our vision to seek the reasons why God's people do what they do. Children are not born angry. Populations of citizens do not spontaneously become angry. Some of the violence that we see is simply a reaction to years of mistreatment and abuse, not just by questionable police actions but by an entire educational and economic system designed to keep a segment of our society poor, illiterate and isolated from the American mainstream. It is easy to react in shock and disbelief at the level of violence that is happening in our city. However, it is another thing to look at the multiple causes of this violence. When we examine these causes, we will not only see the anger of these citizens justified, we may also realize that they are not so different from us. In reality, there is no "us" and "them."

The rioters in the streets are **our** brothers, **our** sisters and **our** children.

Third, we know that God has some experience with bringing order out of chaos. Not so long ago, God took a young Alabama preacher and a tired cleaning woman and started a movement that turned the nation upside down. Dr. Martin Luther King Jr. realized that he was part of the Zeitgeist (spirit of the time), a time when a change needed to happen, and that a new reality would emerge as a result.[21] The ensuing Civil Rights Movement brought much violence, most of it against African Americans, but a new reality did emerge. We were brought a little closer to King's dream of *The Beloved Community*, a dream that would eventually bring us an African American President. We cannot celebrate the Presidency of Barack Obama without acknowledging the sacrifices (many of them ultimate) that put him there. In the same way we should not mourn and be fearful of our present violent times. Our Lord reminds us that new birth arises out of such tumult:

> *Nation will rise against nation, and kingdom against kingdom. There will be famines and earthquakes in various places. All these are the beginning of birth pains.* (Matthew 24:7-8, NIV)

If we who are people of faith believe that God is firmly in control of all creation, we can be assured that God will bring forth a revelation of Divine fashioning and iridescent beauty. That beauty begins when we too disobey the orders of Pharaoh and Herod and let **all** of our young boys truly live! The violent struggles that are now before us are but the

---

[21] John J. Ansbro, *Martin Luther King Jr.: The Making of a Mind* (Orbis Books, 1986) 126.

harbingers of a powerful and unified people, unified in the knowledge of our shared desires for "life, liberty and the pursuit of happiness."

> What, then, is the answer? The answer lies in our willing acceptance of unwanted and unfortunate circumstances even as we still cling to a radiant hope, our acceptance of finite disappointment even as we adhere to infinite hope.[22]

The Rev. Keith O. Paige is Pastor of the 62-member Cherry Hill Presbyterian Church in Brooklyn, a neighborhood in South Baltimore.

---

[22] Martin Luther King Jr. *Strength to Love* (Fortress Press 1963, 1981) 90.

Before It's Too Late

Ronnie A. Hankins

> One of the criminals who were hanged there kept deriding him and saying, "Are you not the Messiah? Save yourself and us!" But the other rebuked him, saying, "Do you not fear God, since you are under the same sentence of condemnation? And we indeed have been condemned justly, for we are getting what we deserve for our deeds, but this man has done nothing wrong." Then he said, "Jesus, remember me when you come into your kingdom." He replied, "Truly I tell you, today you will be with me in Paradise." Luke 23:39-43

As Christ hung dying on a cross at Calvary, a separate story began to unfold there in the midst of this great tragedy. As two convicted criminals hung on crosses next to Jesus Christ, one thief derided Christ wanting to be saved without acknowledgment of Christ's Lordship. But the other criminal, who was convicted of murder and insurrection, makes a revelatory confession of Christ's Lordship and asks Christ to remember him. This criminal was someone who likely had very little and perhaps lived a life surrounded with poverty and crime, yet before he takes his final breath, he realizes his need for a savior; he realizes that only Christ can rescue him from the brokenness of a shattered life and as a result of this criminal's epiphany, a confession of the truth is made thus initiating an act of supernatural engagement which causes Christ to place a momentary pause on his dying process in order to distribute one last gift of unmerited grace for a convicted human being. It's likely that no one cared much for the dying thief; perhaps there were even some who felt he may have gotten what he deserved as a result of the life he led. But despite his shattered life and regardless of whatever crimes he may have committed, the thief made a supernatural request from Christ to be remembered and he received it. Although in the eyes of society this man may have been a wretched and convicted murderer, in the eyes of Christ this thief instantly became a pearl of great price worthy of God's unmerited grace as a result of his acceptance of Christ's Lordship.

Out of this, I see two important points to be made.

1. As human beings, while the blood is still running warm in our veins, it's never too late to come to a revelation concerning the truth of our need for a savior, nor is it too late for God to supernaturally engage a situation with an act of grace and mercy.

2. We should be mindful of how we look upon and judge individuals within our society, remembering that the lens in which society looks at an individual's life is not the same lens to which God looks upon our lives. Where society may see only a thief and a criminal worthy of death, God sees much more and with the power of a simple confession, an act of supernatural grace and mercy is available for anyone who would dare to believe.

On April 12, 2015, Baltimore citizen Freddie Gray is arrested by Baltimore police, and during his arrest, Gray suffers a fatal spinal cord injury believed to have happened while being transported in the back of the police van. A week later after being in a coma for several days, Gray dies at University of Maryland Shock Trauma on April 19th.

The death of Freddie Gray set off continuous and at times violent protests for eight straight days within the city of Baltimore between April 19th and April 26th that eventually boiled over into nationally televised riots on April 27th 2015 and would result in a state of emergency declared by Governor Larry Hogan and a citywide curfew initiated by Mayor Stephanie Rawlings-Blake that would last for several days.

There are arguments on both sides of the justice debate who either feel that Freddie Gray was a victim of the injustice of police brutality and a broken justice system, or that Gray was just another lifelong offender with a long criminal rap sheet and therefore was not worthy of all of the worldwide attention that came about as a result of his unfortunate death. The question remains: as Christian believers, what should we see when we look at each other with the mind of Christ? Much as with the thief on the cross, Christ saw someone completely different from what society saw there on a cross next to him, and likewise we should also be careful not look at each other with tainted lens, but instead with a clear lens of love and compassion.

Through all of what has been endured by our city in the midst of this unrest and anger, I wonder what questions we should be asking ourselves.

- If we as citizens accept and embrace the normalcy of poverty and injustice that exist within our city, should we not also be prepared to accept the precipitation of anger, conflict, mistrust and possible uprisings? It's not too late.
- Will uprisings and unrest become "The New Normal" within U.S. cities across the nation? They very well may be if we as a people do not address

the underlying causes, particularly on issues related to poverty and the lack opportunity for so many within inner city communities around the nation. It's not too late.

Like the convicted criminal on the cross at Calvary, we are in need of an epiphany of truth concerning the realities here within our city and the need for both a deeper and closer relationship with Christ, as well as a need for God's supernatural engagement within our cities and communities, not just here in Baltimore, but across our nation. But it's extremely important to remember that salvation does not come divorced of confessional relationship with God. Like the first criminal in the passage, we cannot scream out for salvation and expect supernatural action from Christ without acknowledging and accepting who Christ is as Lord and Savior. Like the two criminals next to Jesus on the cross, our city is being painfully crucified by our insensitivity to the layers of poverty and injustice which have run rampant through our city for decades; we are being crucified by the disenfranchisement of large groups of citizens who are hopelessly imprisoned by the lack of social and vocational opportunity; we are being crucified by the ever increasing murder rate within our cities by individuals who themselves see little or no value to their lives or the lives of others.

We are being crucified by hopelessness whereby Baltimore has now become the heroin capital, not only here in Maryland, but the heroin capital of the nation. Tens of thousands of people turn to drugs in an attempt to escape the misery associated with not being able to succeed in a society where it seems "only certain people" are able to carve out some sort of path towards a successful life. Yet while the wildfires of poverty, crime, murder, drug addiction, and homelessness continue to burn within our city, other citizens—higher up on the social *promenade deck*—sip margaritas as they separate themselves from the chaos down below on lower inner city levels, not realizing that the entire ship is in danger of being lost, with no apparent escape, upon the high seas of apathy and indifference.

Poverty is a real problem, not only within our city of Baltimore, but also throughout our nation. Many social issues such as violence, murders, and robberies, are precipitants directly related to poverty. However, I believe there are two effective weapons against poverty as expressed through the teachings of Christ.

One is Grace—God's unmerited favor given by God towards us. The cloud of poverty and hopelessness that floats over some areas of Baltimore impacts us all, and the need for grace and mercy on a societal level is imperative if there is to be any change for our current social direction. The apostle Paul wrote in Romans 12th chapter 3rd verse: *For by the grace given to me I say to everyone among you not to think of yourself more highly than you ought to think, but to think with sober judgment, each according to the measure of faith that God has assigned.*

The second lethal weapon against poverty is love. The author of Galatians reminds us to *Bear one another's burdens, and in this way you will fulfill the law of Christ.* (Galatians 6:2)

It's through the activity of God's love that we not only bear one another's burdens, but that we build important relationships amongst one another, which helps to strengthen our communities in ways where we all can prosper and succeed through these difficult times.

Like the thief on the cross, it's not too late to receive a revelation of truth concerning the Lordship of Christ, nor is it too late to ask for Christ's supernatural involvement in the midst of a desperate situation. As Baltimore debates over the guilt or non-guilt of city police officers; as Baltimore removes police commissioners and replaces them with new commissioners; as we invite rock stars such as Prince to come and perform here within the city on behalf of Freddy Gray; as Baltimore politicians argue over whether to add police body cameras to every police officer, or build community centers honoring the life of Freddy Gray; whether we gather 300 men to stand against violence or hold prayer vigils every night against violence and unrest—all of these things have wonderful meaning and significance, but the truth still remains the same: We must address the issue of poverty and do more than just talk about it, but take aggressive action to minimize or even eradicate poverty as being a societal norm within our city. There are tens of thousands of people within our city who are entrenched in poverty and hopelessness. Unless we as citizens begin to understand and take on the burdens of our fellow citizens by addressing the bigger issue of poverty and hopelessness, there will be the continued precipitation of violence and murder within our city, all of which feed the drug subculture and exacerbate the fear and hopelessness felt by so many people.

The number of people standing on corners with cardboard signs (and being ignored) will continue to grow as the societal engine room fires spread quietly throughout the inner city decks below, eventually overtaking our social cruise ship, and unless we take action against this wave of poverty and injustice, much like the doomed Titanic we risk the danger of deep sea peril with nowhere to run or hide upon an ocean of apathy and indifference.

James Baldwin is quoted as saying: *If one really wishes to know how justice is administered in a country, one does not question the policemen or the lawyers, the judges or the protected members of the middle class; one goes to the unprotected—those who precisely need the law's protection the most—and listens to their testimony; ask the wretched how they fare in the halls of justice and you will know not whether or not the country is just, but whether or not it has any love for justice or any concept of it.*[23]

As the riotous fires here with our city are put out, and as broken glass is swept up from our sidewalks and streets, I pray that we as a city would look at Freddie Gray's life as a precious life, even as Christ saw the preciousness of a broken criminal who humbled himself to the Lordship of Christ before it was too late and as a result found his way into Paradise. I pray that we as a society would receive an epiphany of the Lordship of Jesus Christ, recognizing that through sin, we are all criminals and thieves of unrighteousness and therefore need to humble ourselves in submission to God's will for our lives; I pray the we would have the *audacity to believe* in the possibility of God's supernatural ability to engage and impact our city and ask God to remember us even as the thief on the cross asked Christ to remember him as Christ came into his Kingdom.

As a lowly criminal asked Christ to remember, let us also ask Christ to:

- Remember our city and its citizens of all races and ethnic differences.
- Remember the hundreds of homeless people who stand on street corners seeking help.
- Remember those addicted to drugs within our city and those who can only find work selling drugs on corners around the city.

---

[23] James Baldwin, *No Name in the Street* (1972).

- Remember the families of the more than hundreds of lives that were cut short by gun violence within our city.

- Remember each and every one of your servants as we try to bear one another's burdens and live our lives according to your divine will and purpose.

And let us also remember the passage in Matthew 25:31-45.

> When the Son of Man comes in his glory, and all the angels with him, then he will sit on the throne of his glory. All the nations will be gathered before him, and he will separate people one from another as a shepherd separates the sheep from the goats, and he will put the sheep at his right hand and the goats at the left. Then the king will say to those at his right hand, 'Come, you that are blessed by my Father, inherit the kingdom prepared for you from the foundation of the world; for I was hungry and you gave me food, I was thirsty and you gave me something to drink, I was a stranger and you welcomed me, I was naked and you gave me clothing, I was sick and you took care of me, I was in prison and you visited me.' Then the righteous will answer him, 'Lord, when was it that we saw you hungry and gave you food, or thirsty and gave you something to drink? And when was it that we saw you a stranger and welcomed you, or naked and

gave you clothing? And when was it that we saw you sick or in prison and visited you?' And the king will answer them, 'Truly I tell you, just as you did it to one of the least of these who are members of my family, you did it to me.' Then he will say to those at his left hand, 'You that are accursed, depart from me into the eternal fire prepared for the devil and his angels; for I was hungry and you gave me no food, I was thirsty and you gave me nothing to drink, I was a stranger and you did not welcome me, naked and you did not give me clothing, sick and in prison and you did not visit me.' Then they also will answer, 'Lord, when was it that we saw you hungry or thirsty or a stranger or naked or sick or in prison, and did not take care of you?' Then he will answer them, 'Truly I tell you, just as you did not do it to one of the least of these, you did not do it to me.'

It's not too late.

The Rev. Ronnie Hankins, a former Moderator of the Presbytery of Baltimore, is Pastor at Trinity Presbyterian Church, a congregation of 109 members located in Baltimore, very near to where much of the uprising of April 2015 unfolded.

Black Lives Matter

Timothy S. Stern

On the third day there was a wedding in Cana of Galilee, and the mother of Jesus was there. Jesus and his disciples had also been invited to the wedding. When the wine gave out, the mother of Jesus said to him, "They have no wine." And Jesus said to her, "Woman, what concern is that to you and to me? My hour has not yet come." His mother said to the servants, "Do whatever he tells you." Now standing there were six stone water jars for the Jewish rites of purification, each holding twenty or thirty gallons. Jesus said to them, "Fill the jars with water." And they filled them up to the brim. He said to them, "Now draw some out, and take it to the chief steward." So they took it. When the steward tasted the water that had become wine, and did not know where it came from (though the servants who had drawn the water knew), the steward called the bridegroom and said to him, "Everyone serves the good wine first, and then the inferior wine after the guests have become drunk. But you have kept the good wine until now." Jesus did this, the first of his signs, in Cana of Galilee, and revealed his glory; and his disciples believed in him.

After this he went down to Capernaum with his mother, his brothers, and his disciples; and they remained there a few days. John 2:1-12

One hundred and twenty gallons and Jesus was outed in Cana. If you do the math, if you consult your history books and you calculate the size of the six jars at the wedding at Cana, really big jars on hand for the ritual washing of hands before a Jewish meal, then you are astounded to discover the amount of wine that Jesus produced at the matrimonial jamboree. Scholars figure that Jesus conjured up somewhere between 120 and 180 gallons of the good stuff. An incredible abundance for the nuptial feast, Jesus makes a big splash at a local wedding after his mother outs him. The wedding almost crashes but Jesus saves the day and in the words of John reveals his own glory. One wonders why Jesus would make 180 gallons of wine, and Jesus makes himself clear in the Gospel of John Chapter 10 verse 10. "I came that they might have life and have it abundantly."

We live in a land of abundance. We live in a land fiercely committed to the grand experiment of Democracy. We enjoy an un-paralleled religious freedom. We live in a country that has led and continues to lead the world in economics, in technological and medical advances, in entertainment and culture, and in innovations of many kinds. We are the one super power, but we have been outed.

Donald Trump has outed us, candidates who have barely challenged or who support Trump's demagoguery have outed us. The media and certain police officers and police forces have outed us. The racist vitriol against our nation's first mixed race President has outed us. The discouraging enduring and now growing gap between the rich and poor in our country, and entrenched mutigenerational poverty has outed us. Racism is alive and well in our nation, and it walks hand in hand with "White Privilege." Though things have changed dramatically in our nation and much has changed for the better, the headline stories of the last two years have made it clear, that we have much more work to do.

Take the phrase "Black Lives Matter." You can sort of use it as Rorschach test to discover the level of compassion, knowledge and sensitivity there is out there in "White America." The way white Americans react to that phrase tells you something about them/us. The Black Lives Matter people are part of a decentralized civil rights movement with thousands and thousands of differing opinions on the deaths of Black Americans at the hands of police, the racism there is in our criminal justice system, voter suppression in certain states and a host of other issues. Some of the people in the Black Lives Matter movement are legitimately extremely angry about continued racism in our nation and their anger scares certain white Americans. So certain white Americans shout back or at least point out that "white lives matter," "all lives matter," which of course they do. But it's interesting, these white people see the word "only" sitting in front of "Black Lives Matter." That's not what the phrase says. It doesn't say "Only Black Lives Matter" It says simply that "Black Lives Matter." And they do.

They say this because since the creation of our nation and even before our independence, slavery and racism were at our core. We built our democratic empire partially and significantly upon black slavery, the murder and subjugation of Native Americans and upon suppression and discrimination against Hispanic and Asian Americans. Any reading of American History that does not take racism seriously is dishonest. And the reason this is a sermon today is because we claim we are a Christian Nation or a nation rooted in Christian values. Racism is not a Christian value, as Dr. King would remind us.

Jim Wallis, the Director of the Sojourners organization in Washington DC, has just written a new book called *America's Original Sin: Racism, White Privilege and the Bridge to a New America*. In the introduction Wallis quotes Police Commissioner Bill Bratton of New York City as saying at a church breakfast that "many of the worst parts of black history would have been impossible without police." Bratton went on to say at the surprise of Jim Wallis that "Slavery, our country's <u>original sin</u>, sat on a foundation codified by laws enforced by police, by slave-catchers. ... Bratton reminded fellow New Yorkers. that the colonial founder of New York City, the Dutchman Peter Stuyvesant, was a supporter of the slavery system and created a police force to enforce and protect it."[24] Wallis points out that his Sojourners organization first used this phrase "Original Sin" in 1987.

This is what we mean when we use the phrase "Institutional Racism." Our nation's "anti-people-of-color bias" is entrenched in our very culture. And now hundreds of years after colonialism, 250 years after independence, 113 years after the abolition of slavery, 50 years after the first civil rights movement, we still are dealing with an extraordinary unfair criminal justice system that sentences Black People to long prison terms while punishing whites at a lesser level. We are still dealing with poor people and many, many poor black people going to jail because of parking and traffic tickets and unpaid fines; we are still dealing with towns and cities balancing their budget on the backs of the poor. We have politicians ranting against Muslims. We have Trump calling all Mexicans "rapists." It is this kind of bias that can inspire a young white man like

---

[24] Jim Wallis, *America's Original Sin, Racism, White Privilege and the Bridge to a New America* (Grand Rapids, MI: Brazos Press, 2016) xx.

Dylan Roof to go into an AME church and kill nine black people at a Bible Study in Charleston. Maybe it was the Confederate Flag that flew over his State Capital since 1962 in defiance of the civil rights movement. "Heritage not Hate" they say—a profound and astounding lie—institutional hate, entrenched racism, so palpable only a self-deceived person or a liar can deny it.

We are not going to be able to move forward on fairness and justice if we don't speak the truth, if we don't grapple with the concentrated depths of pain and nihilism there is in our Black Urban Communities; where we have by public policy and benign neglect herded people into food deserts, crime traps and gang wars just as we exiled Native Americans to the reservations in the 1800's. And they have not recovered either.

At the suggestion of Pastor Jon and Deacon Linnie Girdner, I read this week some writing by the Baltimore native Ta-Nehisi Coates in *The Atlantic*—an excerpt from his Book *Between the World and Me*. In incredible hauntingly aching words, Coates writes a letter to his teenage son about his childhood in Baltimore, the crime, the gangs and the constant fear in which he lived. And he reflects upon racism in our nation. We all fear that someday ISIS may spring a terrorist attack up on us like in France, Turkey or Pakistan. Coates made me realize that Baltimore African Americans live with real terrorism right now, every day.

Coates says this:

> Here is what I would like for you to know: In America, it is tradition to destroy the black body—it is heritage. Enslavement was not merely the antiseptic borrowing of labor—it is not so easy to get a human

being to commit their body against its own elemental interest. ... At the onset of the Civil War, our stolen bodies were worth $4 billion, more than all of American industry, all of American railroads, workshops, and factories combined, and the prime product rendered by our stolen bodies—cotton—was America's primary export. ... But American reunion [after the Civil War] was built on a comfortable narrative that made enslavement into benevolence, white knights of body snatchers, and the mass slaughter of the war into a kind of sport in which one could conclude that both sides conducted their affairs with courage, honor, and élan. This lie of the Civil War is the lie of innocence, is the dream. Historians conjured the Dream. Hollywood fortified the Dream. The Dream was gilded by novels and adventure stories. ...

Now, the heirs of slaveholders could never directly acknowledge our beauty or reckon with its power. And so the beauty of the black body was never celebrated in movies, on television shows or in the textbooks I'd seen as a child.[25]

I was in the mall yesterday and looking at the advertisements trying to draw me in. All the lightly dressed

---

[25] Ta-Nehisi Coates, "Letter to My Son" in *The Atlantic* July 4, 2015 <http://www.theatlantic.com/politics/archive/2015/07/tanehisi-coates-between-the-world-and-me/397619/>

young white women in the windows. Our culture's definition of beauty is young white thin women.

I have come to believe in these last two years that we need to redefine the American Narrative, we need to correct the myths.

Our nation is a land of abundance, but many people have been left out or left behind. They get little of the abundance that Christ wishes for each of us.

White Christians have a compassion problem. We worry about ISIS and North Korea, but our Black brothers and sisters in Christ live with varied forms of terror every day in this so called land of the free. They tell us they are terrorized but we don't grasp it and we don't have to look at it because we are separate. Do we think they are lying? Some of us do. They are not.

The American Empire was built on slavery and racism. The generational wealth of many White families, white privilege and the accumulated economic power of our nation is partially, even significantly, due to stolen labor. We need to change our narrative. We need acknowledge our indebtedness to slaves.

Slavery was one of our original sins, and its enduring evil legacy persists. Slavery produced Jim Crow, and Jim Crow has not been beaten, it's just sneakier. We cannot run from this. We need to change our narrative; we must tell the story fully and honestly. Racism is so engrained in our national DNA, we who are white do not hardly or fully sense it. We must speak the truth as the truth about Apartheid has been spoken in South Africa.

I am glad to be a part of congregation that is faithful enough to honestly wrestle with these complex and heart breaking issues. I have to admit that when I was reading the Coates excerpt from *The Atlantic*, I found his expression of pain and truth piercing and jarring. It's not easy to let someone's pain and the ache of a people wash over you, but this is what Christ did in his ministry, and this is what we are called to do.

I know that our Christian Ed and Adult Ed team plans classes on this subject after Easter. Perhaps we can have two or three, and I am hoping that as our Long Range Planning Team and our Mission Ministry dream about ministry in our future that the books of Ta-Nehisi Coates and Jim Wallis inform our discerning. Perhaps equipped with compassion and knowledge, we can work with Christ to make our nation a place of abundance for all people.

The Rev. Tim Stern is the founding Pastor of Ark and Dove Presbyterian Church, a congregation of about 275 members in Odenton, MD, about 20 miles south of Baltimore. Tim is a past moderator of the Presbytery of Baltimore.

Hunting for the Kingdom … on the Other Side?

Deborah Ann McEachran

> On that day, when evening had come, he said to them, "Let us go across to the other side." And leaving the crowd behind, they took him with them in the boat, just as he was. Other boats were with him. A great windstorm arose, and the waves beat into the boat, so that the boat was already being swamped. But he was in the stern, asleep on the cushion; and they woke him up and said to him, "Teacher, do you not care that we are perishing?" He woke up and rebuked the wind, and said to the sea, "Peace! Be still!" Then the wind ceased, and there was a dead calm. He said to them, "Why are you afraid? Have you still no faith?" And they were filled with great awe and said to one another, "Who then is this, that even the wind and the sea obey him?"
> Mark 4:35-41

This past week at our presbytery gathering, we were challenged by Rev. J. Herbert Nelson, director of our Office of Public Witness in Washington DC. You may remember him—he is good friends with James B. Parks and preached here at Hunting Ridge one Sunday when I was away. He praised our Presbytery for being willing to confront the issues of racism, classism and poverty, and told us the rest of the denomination was watching us. Because of the unrest last year and the ongoing anxiety about the upcoming trials of the police officers involved in the arrest of Freddie Gray, Nelson noted that if Presbyterians don't move forward in being faithful to God's plan for justice, security, community and healing for all of God's people, God will certainly move on and use someone else to accomplish the plan! He told us this was our time, a unique moment in history. And then he said: "Don't blow it."

Don't blow it. I took that to mean ... Don't get so tied up in internal issues of the church that you forget your calling to go out to serve. Don't get so focused on your own spiritual growth that people could say: "Those Presbyterians—or that church—or that person—they are so heavenly they are no earthly good." Don't miss the opportunity for real change in this city. Don't ignore your neighbors. Don't stop searching for the kingdom. Don't blow it. Nelson describes our work as kingdom work. That is because we are following in the footsteps of Jesus, and his work was to bring in the kingdom of God, not to train the religious establishment, not to pack the pews, not even to grow church membership. Jesus has left us to this kingdom work. On Sunday mornings this Lent we will be unpacking that kingdom work. Where will we find the kingdom? Who makes up the kingdom? And so what is kingdom work?

Some people prefer to avoid the masculine imagery of seeing God as a king who is removed from the common people. Instead they see that our work is to bring in the kindom, that is a world where all of us truly become brothers and sisters, kin to each other. Isn't that what we are looking for in this world of political, racial, economic and gender divides? In this country where leaders are calling for deportation of neighbors and erecting walls? In this city where police officers don't live and there is a place called Jewtown and neighborhoods where whites won't live and others where blacks are still not welcome? We are looking for kinship. Connection. Understanding and recognition. We are looking for God's reign.

Whether it is the Kingdom or Kin-dom, it is not immediately obvious. You cannot draw a line on a map around the reign of God. No political nation can claim to be God's kingdom on earth. There is no visible palace or White House as a seat of power. Jesus describes this kingdom with parables—you know them. The parable of the farmer with his seed, the parable of the lamp under a bushel basket, the parable of the mustard seed. The kingdom grows when the word of God is received and nurtured; the kingdom grows from something very tiny to something very big. After using images to describe the kingdom, he lives out the kingdom of God with his actions.

Imagine after a long day of teaching to a growing crowd of Jews, the sun is going down, and you hear him say: "Let's cross over to the other side of the lake." He is going to head out <u>at night</u> to the other side. Night is the time to shut the door and curl up on the couch with a book. To gather around the table with your family. To rest. Not to leave what is known, what is comfortable, what is familiar. Not to go to the other side. Yet he expects his disciples to go with him. He gives no reason, or at least Mark does not bother to record it. It is the end of the day; this is a clear shift from one kind of teaching to something very new and very different.

You see, the other side of Lake Galilee was a foreign place. It is not home to Jews, but to people who did not share in their faith in God, people who were outsiders, unclean, better left alone. The other side of the lake was Gentile territory. And everyone knew it. Jesus does not just happen to find himself in Gentile territory. He chooses to go to the other side. He is modeling for us what it is to be unharbored.[26] I picked up that image from another preacher, and I share it with you because it is so telling as we go searching for the kin-dom of God. We will not find it if we remain safe and secure in our own harbor, in our own church family, in our own neighborhood, in our own comfort zone. Jesus is unharbored, setting out for the other side. The disciples become unharbored too. Likely more than a little nervously. Likely full of misgivings and doubts—why in the world does he want to mix with "them"? What is going to become of this movement? Other followers cannot really be expected to cross over. They are just too different over there. They won't understand his message. This has got to be a colossal waste of time. Being unharbored is not a comfortable feeling.

When the storm came up, the disciples must have been muttering to one another: "I knew this was not a good idea. We should have stayed home. Now we are all goners. And he is sleeping through it?" Rev. Brian Blount, president of Union Presbyterian Seminary, focused multiple hours of teaching on this one text during the Church Educator's conference downtown a year ago. He pointed out that there is a storm brewing inside the boat as well. It is the storm of fear of the unknown, of discomfort of leaving the predictable, of anxiety of being unharbored, of blaming one another and the sleeping teacher, and the storm of desperation leading to giving up.

Jesus has no intention of letting storms inside the boat or outside the boat keep him from reaching the other side. His kin-dom work is not limited to his neighborhood. It

---

[26] Image borrowed from Rev. Shelli Williams, St Paul's United Methodist Church, Houston, TX.

includes the foreigners on the other side. His work is always to connect rather than divide. Mark describes multiple encounters between Jesus and Gentiles—remember the non-Jewish woman who begged for healing for her daughter? The norms of the day would not have allowed Jesus to reach across the divide between Jew and Gentile. The woman insisted. The woman's faith was unharbored, out in uncharted territory. She knew that there were enough crumbs left to help her daughter. And indeed there were. Jesus heals Gentiles on the other side more than once—removing an unclean spirit on this trip, and then, later in the gospel, restoring hearing and speech to a Gentile unable to communicate. He even duplicated his crowd-feeding miracle on the other side. He fed a crowd of Gentiles, breaking all kinds of tradition, all kinds of religious rules, all kinds of social boundaries.

What is on the other side of the lake for us? Where is a place we avoid? What kind of people do we steer clear of? What are we afraid to talk about? This past week, several of us attended the first of a year-long series of conversations sponsored by the Institute for Islamic, Christian and Jewish Studies here in Baltimore. We heard a Christian perspective first. The next two speakers will bring a Jewish perspective and a Muslim perspective. Then the Institute is calling for a city-wide conversation in small, diverse groups. The whole series is called "Imagining Justice in Baltimore." Right now we have to imagine it. Imagine what this city will be like after the trials of the police officers are over. Will we be a place where God's kin-dom is visible? Will boundaries have been smashed and new relationships formed between people who once lived on the other side? I am not naive enough to think we will repair the broken-ness of centuries in such a short time. But if we do not imagine, if we do not start talking to one another, if we are not willing to be unharbored, we will never reach the other side. Storms come up, both outside and inside the boat. But a storm is not a reason to stay home.

If we are going to hunt for God's kin-dom, we have to get out of the harbor. We have to be willing to go with Jesus to the other side. As unfamiliar as it might be for us, he is already there, already at work, just waiting for us to show up and dig in. What boundary can you break? What conversation can you begin? How do you get involved in the upcoming election process? How do you imagine justice in Baltimore? That is justice for all, not just for some. We can not say, "It is not my problem." As long as justice is missing, it is our problem.

Ready to be unharbored? We have one small opportunity this Lent, to be a part of a weekly small group with brothers and sisters from two other Presbyterian churches—one mostly white and one mostly black. It is venturing out from your own harbor. It is breaking some boundaries. It is crossing over to the other side. I challenge you to commit to a small group—to participate, to listen, to learn. We are in this kin-dom hunt together. We will not find the kin-dom if we stay in the harbor. We must become unharbored. We must cross to the other side. If we don't do it, God will use someone else to get it done. In the words of J. Herbert Nelson: "Don't blow it!"

The Rev. Deborah Ann McEachran is Pastor at Hunting Ridge Presbyterian Church, a multi-cultural congregation of 135 in southwest Baltimore City.

Remember Who You Are
James B. Parks

Now about eight days after these sayings Jesus took with him Peter and John and James, and went up on the mountain to pray. And while he was praying, the appearance of his face changed, and his clothes became dazzling white. Suddenly they saw two men, Moses and Elijah, talking to him. They appeared in glory and were speaking of his departure, which he was about to accomplish at Jerusalem. Now Peter and his companions were weighed down with sleep; but since they had stayed awake, they saw his glory and the two men who stood with him. Just as they were leaving him, Peter said to Jesus, 'Master, it is good for us to be here; let us make three dwellings, one for you, one for Moses, and one for Elijah'—not knowing what he said. While he was saying this, a cloud came and overshadowed them; and they were terrified as they entered the cloud. Then from the cloud came a voice that said, 'This is my Son, my Chosen; listen to him!' When the voice had spoken, Jesus was found alone. And they kept silent and in those days told no one any of the things they had seen.

On the next day, when they had come down from the mountain, a great crowd met him. Just then a man from the crowd shouted, 'Teacher, I beg you to look at my son; he is my only child. Suddenly a spirit seizes him, and all at once he shrieks. It throws him into convulsions until he foams at the mouth; it mauls him and will scarcely leave him. I begged your disciples to cast it out, but they could not.' Jesus answered, 'You faithless and perverse generation, how much longer must I be with you and bear with you? Bring your son here.' While he was coming, the demon dashed him to the ground in convulsions. But Jesus rebuked the unclean spirit, healed the boy, and gave him back to his father. And all were astounded at the greatness of God. Luke 9:28-43

And all of us, with unveiled faces, seeing the glory of the Lord as though reflected in a mirror, are being transformed into the same image from one degree of glory to another; for this comes from the Lord, the Spirit. 2 Corinthians 3:18

In the movie *The Lion King*, Simba, the young lion, runs away after his father, the Lion King, dies. Simba runs both from his past, thinking he is responsible for his father's death, and also from his future as the next Lion King. At some point Simba looks into a deep pool of water and sees his own reflection. When he looks again, Simba's reflection becomes that of his father. His father's image then appears to Simba in the sky, and we hear the unmistakable voice of James Earl Jones saying; "Remember who you are!"

   As we transition from the celebration of the season of the Epiphany to the beginning of Lent, today's text reminds us to take stock of who we are and what it means.

   As is his custom, Jesus went up to a mountaintop one evening to meet God. That, of course, is the purpose of prayer. This time he took three of his disciples with him.

While he was praying, Jesus was visibly transformed. The appearance of Jesus' face changed—that's the word Luke uses—and his clothes turned dazzling white. He is joined by Moses and Elijah, the great law giver and the great prophet.

Luke's gospel tells us that the three discussed Jesus' imminent "departure" at Jerusalem. Now some translations use the phrase "passing" or his "departure." When I was in seminary, my professor pointed out that the Greek word Luke used was the same as the word to describe the Exodus from Egypt. That changes the whole dynamic of the story. This journey to Jerusalem and the events that will transpire there are not about death so much as life. The Easter story isn't about the imprisonment and execution of one man as much as it is about the liberation and redemption of God's creation, including humanity. The Exodus of the people of God from captivity into freedom and fullness of life, which Moses and Elijah began, was finally being fulfilled in Jesus. Israel's covenant to be the people of God on earth came full circle with Jesus.

The disciples, as they often did, had no clue about what was happening. Peter saw the three together, and he naturally wanted to hold on to the moment by institutionalizing it. But before Peter could destroy the power of the situation—you can't control and contain the mystical voice of God—the same voice that spoke at Jesus' baptism said, "This is my Son, my Chosen. Listen to him." Then Jesus stood alone as the one the disciples should listen to. The disciples did not understand that they had been witness to the power of God and how God was using Jesus as the instrument to rescue all of Creation.

This was God's way of telling Jesus, the disciples and Israel to "remember who you are."

While what happened on the mountaintop is important, I think what happened after is just as significant. In the morning Jesus came down from the heavenly glory on the mountain and he was hit with earthly reality. In Mark's account of the events after the transfiguration, the disciples and the scribes were arguing over how to heal a boy who suffered from seizures and convulsions. The disciples, whom Jesus had just days ago given authority to drive out demons, tried, but couldn't do anything for the boy.

Desperate, the boy's father took his child to Jesus. He had to act because while the politicians, academics and so-called experts—oops, I'm sorry—while the disciples and Pharisees argued over who would get credit, over process, over technique, the boy still suffered. Sometimes those of us who sit in comfortable houses and offices pontificating on the best ways to help the poor and the marginalized forget that in the real world people are hurting. Children starve and sick folks die for lack of adequate health care while we talk an issue to death.

After Jesus healed the boy, according to Mark, the disciples asked why they couldn't heal him. Jesus told them that their failure wasn't because of a lack of effort. Their failure wasn't because of technique. It wasn't because of the advice they received. Their failure was because they didn't believe that they needed God's power to succeed. They forgot to pray.

Jesus had only been gone one day and already the disciples had forgotten most of what He taught them. They were attempting, by human effort, to remove a foe that was much more powerful than they were. When Jesus gave them authority to cast out demons, it wasn't in their power but in God's power. Their lack of prayer was typical of their lack of faith. In other words, if they had remembered who Jesus said they were, they would not have forgotten to pray but they would have prayed first. How often do we act first, then after we fail miserably we think about asking God for help?

In the letter to the church in Corinth, Paul says Jesus was not the only one who was changed on that mountain top, Paul says the transfiguration was the basis for all who believe to be led to the knowledge of God.

Listen carefully to Paul's words in this morning's text:

> And all of us, with unveiled faces, seeing the glory of the Lord as through a mirror, are being transformed into the same image from one degree of glory to another; for this comes from the Lord, the Spirit.

Those are powerful words: *All of us... seeing the glory of the Lord as through a mirror, are being transformed into the same image.* Paul is telling us to remember who we are. We are transformed by our encounter with God, just as Jesus, Elijah and Moses were. In this transformation, you don't feel as if you found something; it's more like something found you. Divine love consumes you, and you experience a peace that cannot be explained. You are loved by the creator of Love with a capital "L." God's love lifts the veil from your eyes; it puts to rest your fear of death because you know all things, even death, are in God's hands.

When you are transformed, you realize that you are loved and you are loveable and you become loving. But the strange thing is that you have no control over who you love. All of a sudden you have this desire to and capacity to love everybody: new people, people you already know and even you've never met.

Paul proclaims that Christ sets us free from the Law, but not to do what we want or even to be left alone. We have a covenant with God that we will be the Body of Christ wherever we are, no matter our circumstances. We agree to allow the image of God that is already inside us to shine. No other person in the history of the world is exactly like you. Every person on the planet is a unique creation of God. We also agree to recognize and lift up the unique creation in other people and together to be God's hands and feet in bringing the beloved community into being.

But we have hidden our true identity under a veil of ego, fear and pride. So, instead of being who we were created to be, we spend our lives trying to compensate by worshipping the false god's society pushes on us—power, prestige, possessions, separation from others, abuse of the environment.

Remember who you are.

Jesus commands us to love others, not just feel love. That means we must share God's love with others who are outside our immediate world. To do that means we have to look at the society we live in honestly and admit how the society is structured, especially in ways that favor certain groups of God's children over others.

You can't lose God's love, but you can lose its impact if you don't use it. God freely gives love. It's not earned and it applies to everybody—the beggar on the street, the person who cuts you off in traffic, the gang banger drug dealer, the soldier on the other side of the battlefield, all the Freddy Grays of the world and the police who arrest them, both of whom are trapped in a cycle of violence. God even loves the Pittsburgh Steelers and the New York Yankees. So God's love is not ours to hoard.

Jesus had a special love for those on the margins of society—the poor, the oppressed, the sick, the homeless, the imprisoned. If you think about it, that's who Jesus was in his society. Jesus was a poor Jew, a minority race who lived under the thumb of Roman domination. So the man in whom God entrusted his perfect message was a man who lived on the margins.

How do we, like Jesus, love those who are on the margins? The answer comes from St. Francis of Assisi. According to legend, Francis regarded lepers with disgust as did most everybody. One day when he was traveling, a leper blocked his path. Francis gave the man all his money. The man took the money, but still blocked Francis' path.

Francis then took the cloak off his back and put it on the man's shoulders thinking that would be enough. The man took the cloak, but still did not move. Francis did not know what else to do, so he closed his eyes, braced himself and kissed the man on his diseased lips. When Francis opened his eyes, the man had disappeared. Francis realized at that moment that the man had been Jesus in disguise. From that moment on, he decided to treat every leper as if he were the Christ.

In his book, *The God of Intimacy and Action*, evangelical theologian Tony Campolo asks what would happen if every time we looked into the eyes of someone who is ostracized and oppressed, we saw Christ staring back at us. Campolo says:

> When this is the case, simple acts of charity are not enough. When the Spirit of God moves you to unfathomable depths of love and the suffering of others becomes yours …you will have an irresistibly urgent compulsion to speak on behalf of

those who suffer and to fight for a world that is more just[27].

Too often we just throw money at the poor. That was Francis' first move. Then we figure giving charity—a coat drive, for example—is enough. Francis tried that too. Only when he made the man's suffering his own by kissing the man did he see Christ. Now I am not telling you to go kiss every homeless person or poor person, but I am saying that money and charity are not enough. You must get to know poor people and people of other races as fellow human beings with the same needs and dreams as you have. That requires that you actually come into contact with them, get to know them, respect them, realize their sainthood and finally, take on their suffering as your own. Jesus didn't wait for people to come to his door asking to be healed; he went from village to village seeking those in need.

Remember who you are.

Once you get to know God, you realize that God did not create the mess the world is in today. God did not create war, poverty, racism, greed and class differences. We did and we still do. As the body and mirror image of Christ, we must begin to re-create the society we live in.

Remember who you are.

So what does it mean to be the Body of Christ in Baltimore in 2016? We do what Jesus did. After we spend time with God in prayer and we are transformed, we take the love we have received, share it with others and heal the society around us. But before we can find our true identity,

---

[27] Campolo and Mary Albert Darling, *The God of Intimacy and Action: Reconnecting Ancient Spiritual Practices, Evangelism, and Justice* (Jossey-Bass, 2007) .38.

we must admit who we are and ask God to free us to be who we were created to be. For the Presbyterian Church we love, that means coming to grips with the fact that even though the Census Bureau predicts that this nation will have a majority of people of color in 30 years and although we profess openness and inclusion, our congregations across the denomination are 91.3 percent white. We must grapple with the knowledge that in the Baltimore Presbytery of our six predominantly African-American churches, who are in the middle of the dispossessed that Jesus loved, only two can afford a fulltime pastor or that there is only one person of color on our top governing board, the Steering Cabinet.

Brown Memorial and the rest of the Baltimore Presbytery are blessed to be in a position to be a witness for light in the midst of all the darkness that surrounds us. That's why the Presbytery is taking the entire program year to address the issues of race, class and poverty. We intend to be a long-term force standing for justice, equality and peace in our city. God is moving in our city and our church. Just as the church was the driving moral force behind the Civil Rights Movement we must, once again, be the force that drives a movement for a new normal in America.

Inspired by the love of God for all creation and sustained by our faith, we must be in the front of efforts to say it is a sin that in Maryland, the richest state in the richest nation in the history of the world, more than 243,000 children go to bed hungry every night. It is a sin that if you are born poor in America, you will almost always be poor. A recent Harvard study *Where is the Land of Opportunity?: The Geography of Intergenerational Mobility in the United States*, authored by Harvard economist Raj Chetty, pointed out that the one group that had the worst prospects in life in the entire country is poor black males in East Baltimore.

It is a sin for our nation to absorb more mass murders last year than there were days in the year. It is a sin that that there are more African American men incarcerated in the U.S. than the total prison populations in India, Argentina, Canada, Lebanon, Japan, Germany, Finland, Israel and England combined.

Nobody wakes up each morning wanting to be poor, to be discriminated against, to face a system that is stacked against you, to face the possibility that you may be killed or arrested before the day is over. But we should wake up each day unwilling to accept a society that tolerates poverty, racism, violence. God's children, our brothers and sisters, should not have to live like that, and God's judgement should rain down on us if we don't stand up and do something to change the world we live in.

We all need to look into the mirror of the transfiguration and heed the message Simba was given by the booming voice of James Earl Jones: Remember who you are!

I leave you with the words of Michael Jackson, yes, that Michael Jackson, from his song "The Man in the Mirror":[28]

> I'm gonna make a change
> For once in my life
> It's gonna feel real good
> Gonna make a difference
> Gonna make it right
>
> As I turn up the collar on
> My favorite winter coat
> This wind is blowing my mind

---

[28] "The Man in the Mirror" by Glen Ballard and Siedah Garrett, performed by Michael Jackson on "Bad" CD, 1987.

I see the kids in the streets
With not enough to eat
Who am I to be blind?
Pretending not to see their needs

I'm starting with the man in the mirror
I'm asking him to change his ways
And no message could have been any clearer
If you want to make the world a better place
Take a look at yourself, and then make a change.

If you want to make the world a better place
Take a look at yourself, and then make a change.

Remember who you are.

Remember who you are.

Amen.

Ruling Elder James B. Parks was Moderator of the Presbytery of Baltimore during 2015-16, and is a member of Hunting Ridge Presbyterian Church. These remarks were delivered to the 868th Gathering of the Presbytery of Baltimore, September 17, 2015.

Jesus Wept

Tanya Wade

After he had said this, he went on ahead, going up to Jerusalem.

When he had come near Bethphage and Bethany, at the place called the Mount of Olives, he sent two of the disciples, saying, "Go into the village ahead of you, and as you enter it you will find tied there a colt that has never been ridden. Untie it and bring it here. If anyone asks you, 'Why are you untying it?' just say this, 'The Lord needs it.'" So those who were sent departed and found it as he had told them. As they were untying the colt, its owners asked them, "Why are you untying the colt?" They said, "The Lord needs it." Then they brought it to Jesus; and after throwing their cloaks on the colt, they set Jesus on it. As he rode along, people kept spreading their cloaks on the road. As he was now approaching the path down from the Mount of Olives, the whole multitude of the disciples began to praise God joyfully with a loud voice for all the deeds of power that they had seen, saying,

"Blessed is the king
   who comes in the name of the Lord!
Peace in heaven,
   and glory in the highest heaven!"

Some of the Pharisees in the crowd said to him, "Teacher, order your disciples to stop." He answered, "I tell you, if these were silent, the stones would shout out."

As he came near and saw the city, he wept over it, saying, "If you, even you, had only recognized on this day the things that make for peace! But now they are hidden from your eyes. Luke 19:28-41

War is a terrible thing. No matter how we like to romanticize it, package it, advertise it, or spin it … war is a terrible thing to witness. With that thought in mind … a story is told about WWII, in which Winston Churchill received a call while he was in conference with officials on Downing Street. He was told that an air raid had just occurred. A bomb had been dropped and exploded near his location. It had fallen in one of the poorer sections of London. As soon as he heard the news, Churchill ordered his car to take him to the scene. When they arrived, the sight was heartbreaking, desolation everywhere, homes destroyed, people injured and many killed. The people crowded around Churchill's car and began to cheer. Overwhelmed by this reception, Churchill openly wept. After a bit, a voice from the crowd was heard, saying, "See! he's crying … he really cares about us!"

April 19th marks the one-year anniversary of Freddy Gray's death and the beginning of the unrest that eventually erupted into violence, riots, and an open cry for change on April 27th. Like "War" the event that occurred did not start with the first blow of Freddy's death or the car fires or the destruction of property which are all terrible visual signs of anger, frustration, and perhaps even greed … but in reality, I would venture to say it began with the roots of injustice, inequality, ignorance, mistrust, apathy, treating a whole community as "forgettables," and worthless.

April 19th started out as a beautiful day, a day to spend outside with family and friends, taking a walk, hanging out. … I can imagine that in some ways it was similar to the day that Jesus sent his disciples to prepare for the Passover feast and to locate the donkey he was to ride upon into the city. It was a beautiful day to be outside and to hang out with your friends.

Freddy Gray may not be someone we would call a Jesus-like character, but he was and is a child of God ... someone that God cares about. Like so many other Freddy Grays who yet live in our city ... we must take a look at ourselves and see when, what, where, why, and how God is calling us to interact within this city we call home for our church family. So I will admit that this may seem like an odd way to celebrate and to take notice of Palm Sunday; however, Jesus' action and response in the midst of the celebration calls us to take another look at what Palm Sunday really meant to Him.

The people were going through the normal acts of the Passover celebration. They were rejoicing that the Messiah would come to save them. Yet as they were going through the rituals of the Passover Celebration, they were seemingly unaware of the Spiritual Warfare ... the spiritual battle that was swirling around them. They had missed the cues to fast and pray ... they had missed the cues to full repentance ... they had missed the cues to put on sackcloth and stand humbled before God ... they had missed the cues to listen to Jesus even after God repeatedly proclaimed it with outward and significant acts ... voice from heaven, dove descending, transfiguration, in both instances with a loud voice saying ... Listen to Him. And yet like sheep the people were easily led astray ... by other voices that only sounded pretty important.

So when Jesus fulfilled the words of the Prophet that he would ride into Jerusalem on a donkey, he was not in any way diverted ... nor was his focus redirected to the crowd.

His face had turned to Jerusalem ... his mind was set by the directives of God Almighty ... and yet his heart was filled with compassion for all humanity. Jesus was traveling that day for us, and He had a great vantage point as He rode that donkey down the Mount of Olives toward the city. Jesus even had a great escort as the people shouted with all their might ... "Hosanna! Blessed is He who come in the name of the Lord!" But when Jesus, when he gazed out over Jerusalem he could see more than the beautiful magnificent city. He could see more than the magnificent temple whose roof was covered with gold ... he could see more than the thousands of residents that worked, traded, played, relaxed, worshiped, and lived within its gates. From Jesus' vantage point he could see more ... he could see the spiritual warfare. So instead of focusing on the agenda of the people who were shouting joyful Hosannas, the Word of God says that Jesus wept. Not like he did in John 11 when Lazarus died. In John 11, Jesus shed the kind of tears that well up in your eyes ... overflow and run down your cheeks. These were "dakruo" tears ... he cried in silence. In Luke 19, *Jesus wept* was nothing like that. In Greek the word is "klaio," meaning audible weeping. Jesus was crying like a baby. He cried so hard that He lost control and cried aloud, with visible, audible emotion. In other words, He broke down ... He broke out ... He broke loose with violent gripping passion as He cried over Jerusalem.

    Based on verse 37, I would imagine that Jesus' point of view, His reaction, had to catch the disciples off guard. For the Word of God says that, "Even now at the descent of Olives, the whole multitude of the disciples began to rejoice and praise God." In other words, the disciples were acting happy, shouting and getting caught up in the point of view of the crowd. However, by verse 41 Jesus' point of view and reaction is recorded. Jesus starts crying uncontrollably and those watching had to wonder what was going on in the middle of a good time.

The bottom line is this. From Jesus' vantage point he could see it all ... the beauty of the city, the spiritual warfare, and the future events that were to come, based on hatred, lies, injustice, and the struggle that people deal with every day as sheep being led astray. Yes ... Jesus broke down, broke loose, let it out. Jesus Wept!

In six days ... this, His last visit to Jerusalem, would be over, his suffering, his crucifixion as a criminal, and his death on the cross for the sins of the world. It was going to be devastating! Jesus Wept!

On this Palm Sunday while the people come to church looking pretty, smelling pretty, smiling and rejoicing over the fact that God is "Good" ... do we not see that Jesus is still weeping in the midst of the celebration? Do we not see that Jesus is calling us to care about the condition of our city and the spiritual warfare that continues to rise from under the magnificent city we love? Just as Jesus looked at Jerusalem in the middle of all the wonderful festivities ... can we stop and take a look at the land in which God has called us to be a witness? Jesus asked his disciples to watch and pray ... they were tired and fell asleep. Sometimes it seems like the church has just fallen asleep ... but God calls to us even from the Old Testament in 2 Chronicles 7:14: "If my people, who are called by my name, will **humble themselves and pray and** seek my face **and** turn from their wicked ways, then I will hear from heaven, **and I** will **forgive** their sin **and** will **heal** their land." Jesus wept because we do not trust God in a way that we can truly stand upon the promises of God.

Jesus took the time to stop and look. What he saw made him cry uncontrollable tears with like a baby. Jesus bids us to take a real look ... like the people of His day ... we come waving our palms in celebration, but someone's child has been kidnapped for the purpose of sex trafficking ... it's real and a reality of our world ... Jesus wept about it. We wave our palms in celebration, but someone's brother is hooked on drugs, he is out of his mind drifting in space trying to forget his struggles, his family, his pain, his dilemma, his future, his past, his everything ... it's real and a reality of our world ... Jesus wept about it. We wave our palms in celebration, but someone's sister/someone's daughter is struggling this moment with her children living on the street, sleeping in their car and hoping for Monday to get here quick so that the children can get a decent bite to eat. It's real and a reality of our world ... Jesus wept about it. We wave our palms and dread the direction that your pastor is going with this sermon because she might expect us to touch the untouchable and minister to and with folk who are not like us. It's real and a reality of our world ... Jesus wept about it. We wave our palms while the anniversary of Freddy Gray's death rapidly comes upon us ... reminding us of the unrest and the voices that cry out that Black Lives Matter, Every Life Matters, Every Child Matters, Every Man Matters, Every Woman Matters, Every Community Matters. It's real and a reality that in this world all of these people and places do not matter and for that Jesus wept like a baby!

Jesus wept as he neared the magnificent city of Jerusalem, for within the next six days it would become clear that even His life did not matter to the powers that be on this earth. Perhaps some of the people who shouted "Hosanna, Blessed is He Who Comes in the name of the Lord" were among the sheep led astray, shouting, "Crucify Him! Crucify Him!" Yet in the end ... Jesus' life was the only life that mattered, for His was the life that gave life … brought God's loving compassion to humankind … for God so loved the world that He gave …

From Jesus' point of view … He has done more than talk Himself blue … Jesus has given His life for us and bids us to take that step of faith … to make a decision, one that will change the direction of our lives … change the direction of our focus. It all begins by asking Jesus into your life as Lord who forgives and saves.

How many of you remember the Bay Bridge between San Francisco and Oakland during the World Series where the upper section collapsed on the lower one? There was a man who was frantically waving his arms, trying to get oncoming traffic's attention, trying to let them know about the danger waiting ahead. But some kept on driving, a few were rude to him making negative gestures and yelling at him, but as they went past him, their cars went off the edge of the bridge to their death, although they did not initially understand why the man wanted them to stop. There were others who took the time to stop, look and listen to the man's warning. Once they realized what he was trying to do they understood and to this day they are forever grateful for his caring heart.

Jesus looked over Jerusalem and wept, for he saw those who choose the way of the world over the kingdom of God putting their very souls in jeopardy. Yet God calls us the body of Christ to care … even when people reject us like they rejected Him … we are a part of God's plan to plant the seeds that shall produce fruits of the spirit.

There was a story shared about a young boy who was embarrassed by his mother's appearance when he was growing up. She seemed to own only two dresses and never spent any money on herself for new shoes, make-up, or any of the things he thought would make her presentable. Later, he learned she did what she did, wore what she wore, put up with the teasing and ridicule she experienced, so that HE could wear new clothes, have the latest toys, so that HE might not be made fun of at school. Once he understood that, he found her appearance something he was very proud of, because now he "got it." She did what she did because she loved him ... even when he didn't appreciate her love.

Jesus looked out over Jerusalem and wept because He possessed the same love for us, that unconditional love that will give up everything even for those who do not understand. Jesus wept like a baby for His disciples and all of us who call upon the name of the Lord that we too might look at the city of God from God's vantage point and act in love and compassion for all of humanity.

(Luke 19:41ff) And when He approached, He saw the city and wept over it, saying, "If you had known in this day, even you, the things which make for peace!" To the glory of God, we pray. Amen.

The Rev. Tanya Wade is Pastor at Grace Presbyterian Church, a congregation of 182 in northwest Baltimore City. She was the first African American woman to be ordained in Baltimore Presbytery.

From Hope to Wholeness
Mary D. Gaut

> Let us hold fast to the confession of our hope without wavering, for he who has promised is faithful. And let us consider how to provoke one another to love and good deeds, not neglecting to meet together, as is the habit of some, but encouraging one another, and all the more as you see the Day approaching. (Hebrews 10:23-25)

This ancient admonition is written to a group of early Christians whose commitments and enthusiasm had begun to wane. They had become sluggish and uninspired. The one who writes is eager to give them a spiritual and theological pep talk, hoping to rekindle among them a renewed passion for who they are called to be and what they are called to do.

One year ago, our city was awash with violent protests following the funeral of Freddie Gray. The pain that had long simmered in the neighborhoods, where institutional racism and systemic poverty and neglect had all but wiped out hope, boiled over in violent protest. Where were you on that night?

I would not presume to speak for all of you gathered here, but I imagine many if not most were where I was: watching the continuous news coverage on TV from the relative comfort of our homes, most likely some "safe" distance from where the riots were taking place. We couldn't pull ourselves away from the screen, could we? From our family rooms we got a pretty good sense of what was going on. But we began to wake up to realities we had preferred not to notice. We began to notice how great was the distance that existed between us and what was happening on the streets near the North Avenue CVS and Mondawmin Mall.

A few miles might as well have been a few hundred or thousand miles. We could watch. But if we were not there, we did not hear the shattering of glass and the pounding of boots running down the street. We did not smell the smoke or feel the heat of the fires. We watched from a *safe* distance. We heard news crews describe things for us. We watched the flames and heard the shouts through the mediated perspective of a television camera. Even though this was our town, we were not there. Though we may have driven along many of those streets before, we really didn't know those neighborhoods or the people who lived there. In spite of the marvels of technology that allowed us to watch the uprisings in real time, the boundaries that existed between us and those on the street that night were almost insurmountable. They had existed for a long time. For generations, we had carefully, if not consciously, kept our distance. The unbearable reality that too many endure had become, for many others, another reality show. We could avoid responsibility by simply changing the channel.

Tonight we are gathered for worship around the theme "from hope to wholeness." We have a sense of what wholeness might look like for Baltimore and beyond. Yet, so far it has remained only a hope. And hope alone is not sufficient for the magnitude and complexity of the issues before us. It has been too easy for many of us to remain remote and aloof from the pain, conveniently removed from the effects of institutional racism and poverty—

preaching and praying for justice and wholeness but rarely examining our own complicity in the injustices and the brokenness.

This is a critical moment in our city as well as our nation, when our religious institutions are called to a new level of involvement ... to a familiarity with our neighborhoods and our neighbors unfiltered by the prejudices, technologies and policies that have, for too long, kept us apart. This is the moment when we must come together and bring the voice of moral urgency to the issues before us.

Hope for a just and whole tomorrow can no longer be a private prayer. It must become a public passion ... a job description shared by those of us who have more social, political and financial capital than we want to admit. Therefore, as the text reminds us, *let us consider how to provoke one another to love and good deeds.* Let us reorient hope from passive waiting to active involvement that moves us, in visible and tangible ways, toward wholeness.

The Rev. Mary D. Gaut is currently the Interim General Presbyter of the Presbytery of Baltimore. These remarks were delivered at the Interfaith Prayer Service at the Basilica of the National Shrine of the Assumption of the Blessed Virgin Mary, April 25, 2016, commemorating the one-year anniversary of the uprisings.

www.ingramcontent.com/pod-product-compliance
Lightning Source LLC
Chambersburg PA
CBHW071924290426
44110CB00013B/1467